Black and White Sands

Black and White Sands

A bohemian life in the colonial Caribbean

ELMA NAPIER

PAPILLOTE PRESS
London and Trafalgar, Dominica

First published in Great Britain in 2009
Reprinted 2014

© 2009 for the estate of Elma Napier

A CIP catalogue record for this book is available from the British Library.

Typeset in Sabon

Design by Andy Dark
Cover design by Andy Dark, adapted from a vintage Royal Mail line poster by
Kenneth Shoesmith

ISBN: 978 0 9532224 4 5

Papillote Press
23 Rozel Road
London SW4 0EY
United Kingdom
www.papillotepress.co.uk
and Trafalgar, Dominica

ACKNOWLEDGEMENTS

The publisher would like to thank the family of Elma Napier, in particular Patricia Honychurch and Lennox Honychurch for their permission to publish the book, and for their unstinting support, wealth of knowledge and generosity; also many thanks to Michael and Josette Napier for their help, in particular for the loan of photographs, and to Alan Napier likewise. Thanks, too, to Margaret Busby, for the index. All photographs, unless otherwise credited, are courtesy of the Honychurch and Napier families.

BY THE SAME AUTHOR

Nothing So Blue (1927)
Duet In Discord (1936)
A Flying Fish Whispered (1938, republished by *Peepal Tree Press*, 2009)
Youth Is A Blunder (1948)
Winter Is In July (1949)

Contents

Dominica

Map of Dominica showing the main places mentioned in this book, parish boundaries and the extent of motorable roads on the island before 1956. The parishes of St. Andrew and St. David made up the constituency of Lennox and Elma Napier in the Legislative Council.

Before Dominica:
a portrait of
Elma Napier

*Elma Gordon
Cumming as a
child in Scotland
in 1899.*

"I have made of my life a curious patchwork," wrote
Elma Napier. Indeed, by the time she arrived in Dominica
with her husband and children in 1932, this talented and
fearless woman had spent her childhood on a grand estate in
the Scottish highlands, lived in the Australian outback,
visited the South Seas, and danced with the future Edward
VIII. More significantly, she had emerged from two
scandals: the social ostracism of her aristocratic father from
the Edwardian court, and her own adultery and divorce.
Such emotional upheavals she never mentions in Black and
White Sands but they shaped her life, and, ultimately,
brought her to the wild tropical shores of Dominica where
she lived until her death in 1973 at the age of 81.

Elma Napier was born in Scotland, the eldest child of Sir
William Gordon Cumming, whose family had owned "half
of Scotland", including the house that later became
Gordonstoun school. But in 1890, two years before her

birth, Sir William was accused of cheating during a baccarat game with the Prince of Wales (later King Edward VII). This famously became known as the Tranby Croft affair. Sir William sued for defamation, and lost. He also lost his place in high society, and was, for ever after, shunned. "No one spoke to him," wrote his daughter of her father's disgrace.

But Elma was to suffer more from being born a girl ("It was understood in our house that boys were superior beings") than from social rejection. She was a teenager when she realised her function was to make a brilliant marriage and so help rehabilitate the family. Her first memoir, Youth

Family group at Hopeman House, Morayshire, Scotland, in 1927. Elma is in the front, with daughter Patricia on her knee. Back row: left, Sir William Gordon Cumming (father) and Alastair (brother). Middle row (left to right): Betty (sister-in-law) with her daughter Josephine; Cecily (sister), Daphne (daughter) and Roly (brother).

is a Blunder, of her early years, evokes what she called the "casual cruelty of childhood" often confined to a lonely existence with governesses (and 30 indoor servants), and only leavened by her love for exploring moors, forest and sea. She felt disconnected to her background, wanting to "run like a hunted hare" because, as she said, she felt that she "heard a different drummer".

Then, at 18, she fell in love with a married man. When her parents found out, her mother told her "no decent man will marry you now". But her mother was wrong, because a year later, she gratefully married Maurice Gibbs, an upper-class Englishman with global business connections. For nine years the couple lived in Australia, which she loved for its freedom and landscape, for a time on a sheep station exploring by car, horse and on foot the continent's ferocious environment. Even so, she felt constrained by wifely duties.

Then she met Lennox Napier. He was also English, and also a businessman, but he had progressive ideas and had lived among the artists of post-Gauguin Tahiti: he introduced her to books and paintings and "the world that reads the New Statesman". At first, as she wrote, she "had soft-pedalled this invitation to the waltz" but their relationship deepened. And in this partnership she found an answer to her restlessness. But it was at a high cost. In the wake of her divorce, she forfeited the two children of that marriage into the care of their father. (Ronald became an RAF pilot and was killed in action in 1942, while daughter Daphne would eventually rejoin her mother and, aged 20, accompany the Napiers to their new beginning in Dominica.) Elma and Lennox married in 1924.

The couple had "discovered" Dominica on a Caribbean cruise – taken on account of Lennox's fragile health – and "fell in love at first sight, an infatuation without tangible rhyme or reason, yet no more irrational than any other falling in love". At that time, it was dismally poor, sunk in colonial neglect. Indeed, some historians have argued that the small islands of the Caribbean had remained essentially unchanged since the end of slavery. But as Elma Napier evokes in Black and White Sands, her memoir of her life on the island, this was a society characterised by a self-sufficient peasantry, free to work the land and sea, unhindered by authority, and possessing a rich Creole culture. Peasant lives changed little until, after the shortages and dramas of the war years, post-war reforms brought roads, universal suffrage and some redistribution of land to this mountainous and dazzlingly green island.

Elma and Lennox Napier both played a part in these changes, in the politics of their adopted island. They may have been upper-class bohemians — complete with servants, but they were not lotus-eaters, nor, indeed, were they like the sybaritic settlers of that more famous part of empire, Kenya's Happy Valley. Both became, at different times, members of the colony's Legislative Council, Elma being the first woman to sit in a Caribbean parliament. Many years later this achievement was celebrated on a Dominican stamp that bears her image.

The Napiers, with their two small children, Patricia (Pat) and Michael, settled about as far away as was possible from the island's capital Roseau. They lived in the north-coast village of Calibishie, building their house, Pointe Baptiste,

Captain Lennox Napier during the first world war, with his pet lion cub, at a field hospital in France while recovering from his wounds. He married Elma Napier in 1924.

on a cliff between two beaches – one of black sand, the other of white sand, and hence the title of this book. While they were certainly the "Sir" and "Madame" of the Big House, and ordered crystallised fruit and pâté from Harrods, they had different horizons from the rest of Dominica's small white population – mainly colonial service officials whose wives wore gloves for tea parties, and played tennis at the all-white club.

Elma Napier did not do that: with upper-class élan, she swam in the nude, walked alone along forest trails and endured long horseback rides to remote villages in tropical downpours. While the other wives baked cakes and gossiped about the servants, Elma wrote articles for the Manchester

Elma Napier

Guardian, talked to men about politics and learned about the landscape and culture of her adopted island.

The latter was very important to her. "I would rather be an explorer to see round the next corner than anything else except a fluent writer," she once wrote. Elma Napier flourished in Dominica: it excited her sense of adventure, her curiosity about its people, and her love of wilderness. An early environmentalist, she fought to preserve the island's great forest ranges, and describes its ecology with an eager eye – from the delights of birdsong and rare orchids to the horrors of cockroach and termite.

Lennox died in 1940, only eight years after their arrival. Elma remained at Pointe Baptiste with its dark glowing furniture, painted screens and books. She continued in her role as hostess – welcoming passing visitors, grand and not so grand, to elegant lunches, although leaving the cooking to the servants. Somerset Maugham, Noel Coward, Patrick Leigh Fermor and Princess Margaret had all sat on that deep veranda with its ever-changing views of mountains and sea.

While life in Dominica became somewhat more prosperous by the 1950s with the arrival of the banana boom, life at Pointe Baptiste remained the same. Elma Napier refused to have a radio – it was the servants who brought her news about the outside world. She said that a "typewriter, pen and sewing machine" were all the moving parts she required. There was no electricity – as the sun began to set beyond the great silhouette of nearby Morne Diablotin, lamps were lit. Once, interviewed by BBC Woman's Hour about life in Dominica, she had piled on "the discomforts, the oddities" and told her audience about sleeping in police stations where the rats took her food. Being courted by Lennox with a picnic of champagne and gardenias, she wrote that she would have been just as happy with "three ham sandwiches and a bar of chocolate". There was an appealing no-nonsense, lack of sentimentality to her character, which explains perhaps her ability to flourish in the dynamics of island life at that time.

Dominica has produced two other important women writers, both of the white plantocracy: Jean Rhys and Phyllis Shand Allfrey. Rhys and her husband, the publisher Leslie Tilden-Smith, came to tea at Pointe Baptiste in 1936, but Elma Napier talked books with Tilden-Smith rather than with Rhys, and when Wide Sargasso Sea was published 30 years later, she did not recollect their meeting. She had, perhaps, more in common with Allfrey, also a politician, but although they applauded each other's work, the two women rarely met, living at opposite ends of the island.

Elma's first book, of travel sketches, had been published in 1927. There were two novels, published in the 1930s, both set in Dominica: A Flying Fish Whispered (which is to be re-published by Peepal Tree Press), and Duet in Discord. Then came a gap until two memoirs: Youth Is A Blunder (1948), and Winter Is In July (1949) largely about her life in Australia. Black and White Sands was written in 1962, but has remained unpublished until now.

Elma's death came in 1973, and she is buried, alongside her husband by the track that runs from Pointe Baptiste towards Black Beach. The house itself remains in the family, but is now a holiday rental. Her family continues to contribute to island life: Daphne lives with her family in Dominica, as does Elma's younger daughter, Patricia, whose son, Lennox Honychurch is a historian and anthropologist. Other grandchildren and great-grandchildren also live and work in Dominica, the island of which Elma wrote: "It has never been easy to analyse, to define the mysterious charm that has lured some people to stay in Dominica forever, and from which others have fled without even taking time to unpack." Elma Napier stayed forever. Black and White Sands is the fruit of that experience.

Polly Pattullo

1 | Falling in love

The ship quivered to the wind in the channel. Spray spattered on to the main deck. There was a smell of rubber; a whiff of oil. Far astern the volcano of Martinique hung like a pale triangle between sea and sky. I heard the French consul general say to the lady from South Carolina: "It appears that in Dominica my subordinate is a man of colour. It will not be possible for my wife to go ashore." And the lady, who wore black kid gloves and a lace veil covering an immense hat, sympathetically concurred.

From the north, dark and clouded mountains were already bearing down upon us with a strange effect of haste, of almost sinister import. Surf reared itself against impassive cliffs to fall back defeated. Vegetation clogged the valleys, shrouded the hills. Not until we were close inshore was there sign of human habitation; a tin roof, a spire, brown houses on stony beaches.

The ship cast anchor off the town of Roseau. Men dived

from rafts for "black pennies", the pale soles of their feet waving in the water like seaweed. There was a clamour of boat owners. "Take Victoria, Mistress." "Master, White Lily for you." Buildings with shabby faces lined the bay front. Small fish were making seemingly aimless excursions under a jetty of wooden piles encrusted with sea eggs and barnacles. We sought the Botanical Gardens, and were pestered by small-boy beggars and would-be guides who led us through cobbled streets where wooden houses were mounted on massive foundations. Here and there one might glimpse a courtyard where vines were spread on a pergola behind a sagging mansion. A rampart of cliff overhung three cemeteries wherein the dead of three denominations were blanketed in pink coralita and croton bushes.

Under mahogany trees on a velvet lawn the matron of the hospital routed the little boys. "If you follow that path," she directed, "you will come to the Morne barracks." Already, our breath had been taken away by the beauty of the flowering shrubs. "Look at this one," we cried. "What is that?" Climbing the zigzag path, we stopped at corners to look down on to the red-roofed town and the shining sea, and came at last to a shrine under a talipot palm where the image of Christ was nailed among pointed stakes. At the foot of the cross, tight bunches of oleanders had been thrust into jam jars between lighted candles whose flames were quenched by the afternoon sun. A coloured woman, wearing a silk dress and head kerchief, knelt in prayer. Behind her, an ancient cannon, half buried in the grass, lay as though overthrown by the prince of peace.

Beyond a plot of young lime and orange trees, we found

*Lennox and Elma
Napier in 1932
shortly after arriving
in Dominica –
"With Dominica we
fell in love at first
sight, an infatuation
without tangible
rhyme or reason".*

the barracks; stone buildings, three of whose roofs were rusted to the colour of mango flowers while the fourth was altogether missing. They were set square about what had once been a parade ground. There was an old man mowing the lawn and the lazy sound of his machine carried all summer in its droning, so that one could almost smell English grass. He said: "Self-help, Sah? Over there." And then, feeling perhaps that he had coped inadequately with the sudden appearance of strangers, he removed a tattered straw hat and, wiping his forehead with his arm, said: "Here walk the headless drummer."

Suspecting that we had strayed into the local loony bin we approached the best repaired building and there

The Roseau valley – a typical Dominican landscape of river, mountain and forest.

discovered a little old white lady who sold us rum punches in a bare room with tables. There were postcards for sale and bead necklaces; gourds made into rattles with painted faces, and coral fans which – when alive and rooted – sway on the surface of the sea like the fins of sharks. "Government allows us to use this room for the ladies self-help association," said the diminutive person. I could not refrain from asking: "Help themselves to what?"

Therefore it had to be explained that ladies who made jam, or bottled cashew nuts, or did embroidery, might here sell their wares to tourists. But neither my husband Lennox nor I were listening any more: far away up the valley, a waterfall poured out of a black-grey mountain whose summit was hidden in cloud. The veranda rail was wreathed in yellow alamanda, and white flowers shaped like trumpets.

"What a wonderful place to live," I muttered.

And the little old lady in the guise of Lucifer whispered: "You might rent the other room to sleep in. It would be very primitive. We don't have many tourists in Dominica."

"What did the old boy mean about the headless drummer?" Lennox asked.

And she said: "Oh, there's an old legend from the French wars," she smiled. "He wouldn't trouble you."

Back on the boat that evening, with the moon rising behind the mountains, dinner was eaten to the sound of waltzes and musical comedy selections in a brightly lit salon where the French consul general was seated with a pale and attractive young man who, in a few weeks would be our solicitor. The lady from South Carolina had made acquaintance with a beautiful blonde whose yellow dress and yellow hair had struck me all of a heap across the crowded room.

"But who is she?" I asked the chief engineer, "Who can she be?"

An American, I was told, resident in the island, living among oranges in the high hills in an estate called Sylvania.

"Tell me," a fellow passenger was saying, "How do you manage here, you a southern girl, meeting coloured people? Do you shake hands?"

And the blonde laughed with a touch of defiance. "Of course," she said, "I've done more than that."

Thus for the second time in one afternoon, although for the first time in our lives, we met this odd differentiation between persons known as the colour bar, against which we

Holly Knapp on a garden swing at La Haut. Lennox Napier and Holly Knapp had become friends in Tahiti after the first world war, and met up again by chance in Dominica.

immediately flung ourselves to break it down. ("I tell you they are giants," said Don Quixote of the windmills. "And I shall fight against them all.")

Later, on deck, the same blonde was heard asking someone from the shore, "Who is staying at the Paz Hotel nowadays?"

"There's an American called Knapp from Fiji, I think," was the answer whereupon my husband broke excitedly into the conversation. "Knapp?" he said, "with a red beard?" Lennox had known John Holly Knapp 13 years previously in Tahiti, which in this place might easily be confused with Fiji. And instinctively he knew that it must be the same man: the Knapp whose house he had helped to build in Taravao; the Knapp who would not write letters and so lost touch with his friends; the Knapp of whom Frederick O'Brien had written in Mystic Isles of the South Seas: "Without doubt as near to a Greek deity in life, a Dionysus, as one could imagine.... red-gold beard, dark curls over a high forehead, two flaming hibiscus blossoms behind his ears."

As the Lady Drake was about to sail for Montserrat, Lennox sent a card ashore by the agent, writing on one side of it: "You must be my old friend whom I am sorry to have missed seeing," and on the other: "My wife and I plan to come back in three weeks' time." It was typical of Holly that, on receiving the card, he should have looked at one side only, grieving loudly and bitterly at not having seen Lennox, sticking the evidence into his mirror, until days later, his friend Lorna Lindsley idly removed it and, turning it over, exclaimed: "But they're coming back."

That first visit to Dominica was in the winter of 1931. In the autumn of that year we had been living in London with our two children and the grown-up daughter of my first marriage. It was the depression, and Lennox was overtired, overworked, and constantly rather ill. Both of us on the brink of 40, we seemed to be settled and sunk in domesticity, less well-off than we had been, and seeing little prospect of further adventure. Then a lung specialist, stating positively that Lennox showed no evidence of tuberculosis, nevertheless recommended that we take three months' holiday in search of sunshine, and we chose to go to the West Indies because we knew so little about them.

Between Christmas and New Year we sailed from

England for Trinidad in the French ship Colombie, then making her second voyage, and from Port of Spain we took the Canadian national steamship Lady Drake north through the Windward and Leeward islands. Dominica was the only island for which we had no letters of introduction, and with Dominica we fell in love at first sight, an infatuation without tangible rhyme or reason, yet no more irrational than any other falling in love.

When we returned to Dominica – as we had promised ourselves – three weeks later, we climbed into the Paz Hotel by a steep and narrow staircase leading straight off the street into a parlour crowded with basket chairs. Faded and worm-eaten photographs decorated the walls. A tight bunch of croton leaves had been thrust into a brass bowl. Conscious of my hot and crumpled appearance – we had left the pension in Martinique at five that morning and travelled second class in a horrid ship – I went out on to a balcony from which one looked down on to ruined walls. A man and a dog slept side by side on the pavement; a child carried a hand of ripe bananas on her head. Behind the town, mountains were cut into a blue-black frieze against rain clouds.

And there in the Paz was Holly. Attired in a well-fitting white suit with no hibiscus behind the ears, he was not quite my idea of Dionysus. His beard was red indeed but silvered rather than gold. Thus, with mutual pleasure, a friendship made in Tahiti was renewed in the West Indies in 1932.

With Holly that morning in the Paz were Percy Agar, who was to become my son-in-law, and Paul Ninas, an American artist who had lived for three years in the north of Dominica and who, summoned home on account of his father's mortal illness, had lent his house to Holly. It is funny, remembering my shy flight on to the balcony, to realise that Holly and Lorna thought me too "ladylike" to come camping with them in the rough house built by Paul near Calibishie village; and it was not until Lorna had left the island that the invitation was extended which was to change our lives.

Meanwhile the self-help ladies provided beds, knocked a few nails into a wall, and installed us in two rooms in the old barracks. There were no mosquito nets and we slept badly. "They are only bush mosquitoes," the ladies said, "they won't do you any harm." I looked ruefully at my swollen arms and decided harm had been done. From then on we burned coils of incense which looked like cobras ready to strike and made the room smell like a French church.

The ladies also produced Sarah, an ugly woman, a Seventh Day Adventist, and not a very good cook. On the first evening, she had served dishwater soup and a casseroled chicken cunningly designed to be all bone and no flesh. "It's a knack peculiar to 'other races'," Lennox said. "I remember a Chinese cook in Apia..." And I retaliated with a description of a fowl mangled on a lakeside under Fujiyama. Sarah craved permission to go down the hill to Roseau. "I look for a boy to sleep with me," she said. In view of her unprepossessing appearance I could only wish her luck with a touch of pessimism. Next morning, a spindle-legged child of 10 emerged from the kitchen. "He my son," Sarah announced proudly.

May, the messenger, was plump and strong, smiling, and perhaps 17. Returning from town with a basket of vegetables upon her head crowned by a block of ice wrapped in a sack, she would stand by the veranda rail asserting with proud simplicity, "I back." And indeed it seemed to me that she had reason for pride, for the hill was steep and the load heavy; and I felt slightly ashamed for lying in a deck chair alternately studying Dominican history and throwing bread pellets to lizards. But anyone living so vitally in the present as May would not in the least have cared that battles long ago had been fought in this place, and she would know that lizards – "leezards" – did not require bread.

From one veranda we could see the roadstead streaked with pale currents and dotted with the sails of fishing boats; and from the other the Roseau valley ending in Morne Micotrin whose triangle, at sunrise, would be blackly outlined against a pink sky. At midday, with the peak wreathed in clouds, rainbows would play upon the little village perched on its shoulder. But at sunset, when light filled the dark gullies and the creeper-hung recesses, then the valley would yield its secrets – steam rising from the sulphur springs; patches of the most delicate green sugarcane, lime trees, destined to produce Rose's lime juice cordial, and always the silver ribbon of the waterfall pouring, so it seemed, out of nothing into nowhere.

Beyond the barracks, a path trailed into a scrubby forest where a stream was clouded with a grey stain as though smoke were held under the surface of the water; and, where it dawdled among huge leaves there was an orange scum, sinister and mephitic. A broken-down hut was rotting in that place, under slimy moss; and a tree fern had pushed off the roof which lay dismembered in the undergrowth. Sadness and decay, a flavour of old, unhappy far off things, underlay the island's beauty. It has never been easy to analyse, to define the mysterious charm that has lured some people to stay in Dominica forever, and from which others have fled without even taking time to unpack.

We made excursions on horseback hiring quadrupeds from the barber, crossing the backbone of the island by way of a crater called the Freshwater Lake to distinguish it from the Boiling Lake. For days we climbed precipitous ridges or followed red clay tracks within reach of the Atlantic spray; rode through deep forest, silent save for the call of birds; heard for the first time the unhappy note of the *siffleur montagne*; and forded again and again swift mountain streams, or broader, smoother ones where every day seemed

The bay front, Roseau, Dominica's capital, as it might have looked in the 1930s. Mural by Elma's grandson, Lennox Honychurch.

to be washing day, and garments too torn to be identified, too faded for the original colour to be recognised, were spread on stones too hot for the hand to touch.

Later, we were rediscovered by the American blonde, Patsy Knowlton, whose preoccupation with new people had brought the name of Knapp into the conversation, and one day, we went to see her and her husband John at Sylvania. We drove on a rough metalled track called the Imperial Road because it had been given to the island in celebration of Queen Victoria's diamond jubilee. Purple bougainvillea marked the entrance to an old stone house under a saman tree. A broken aqueduct, spotted with ferns and moss, carried water to turn a wooden wheel attached to some invisible machinery. On a narrow col between two watersheds, there was a long low house facing a stupendous panorama of hill and forest which, as clouds passed over, was cut into ever-changing shapes of blue and purple and black.

"Come and look at Morne Diablotin," said John. "You may never have another opportunity." And although I have had countless opportunities, I still remember the mountain as it was that day, blue with a touch of sunset gold on it.

"We've only been here two years," they told us, growing oranges commercially. And the first thing that happened was a hurricane. There were photographs taken before the disaster and after when trees lay on the ground and stripped branches cried for vengeance. We understood then why the people of Dominica were so hurricane conscious. Yet already, where destruction had been, we saw hibiscus hedges, gardenias and a white beaumontia vine writhing among the tree tops.

At Sylvania, where we stayed for a few days, small black finches with red breasts would perch on our beds in the mornings, and at the breakfast table would peck the butter, mangle the toast. Sometimes, towards evening, the mountain called Trois Pitons would flame as though it were on fire, and then bats would fly from under the veranda roof in a great cloud and, dispersing into the twilight, be seen no more.

With Holly and Lorna, we walked from the barracks at Morne Bruce to the village of Giraudel. We sat to eat our lunch under a wayside Calvary, such as one might see in Brittany, the figure of Christ on his cross, with a saint on each side. Children brought us, on plates made of banana leaves, *fwaises* which are not strawberries nor yet quite raspberries, but which grow wild on that side of the island and, like the edible frog called *crapaud* or mountain chicken, do not cross the dividing range. This area near Giraudel is a dry part of the country, the steep watercourses standing empty, and we were glad when people brought us drinking water in red clay goblets, not realising then how very far they had had to carry it, bringing it up in buckets or kerosene tins from the valley half an hour's climb away.

At Gomier, the estate of a family named Honychurch, we found three white children swinging on a bamboo stem, one of whom, 20 years later, would marry my younger daughter. Their red-haired mother, who had brought up nine on rather less than the proverbial shoestring, was occupied in writing a piece for the Dominica Chronicle replying for the defence to a priestly condemnation of strange women who walked about the island without stockings.

Percy Agar had sent his overseer to meet us at Gomier that he might show us the cross-country way to his home at La Haut. A huge negro, inappropriately called Cheri, he was naked to the waist, swinging a cutlass, and carrying a bundle suggestive of a severed head dripping blood, which was no more than Lorna's wet bathing suit done up in a red handkerchief. He led us by a steep path to the La Haut river, almost choked with a white wild ginger, very sweet smelling; and, having crossed over, we came into Percy's cocoa cultivation – a darkness studded with red and purple and golden pods hanging on thin trunks. It was a long climb up the hill to the lawn under saman trees. It had been a long day.

I lay full length on the veranda and Percy made rum punches for us of whose potency – until I tried to get up – I was unaware (although I felt better for drinking five). A scarlet passion flower enveloped the veranda rail. Little birds called *rossignol* nested in a box. There was no motorable road to the house. One walked the stony trail between sandbox trees and *savonette*, *coubaril* and bay. And when we tried to order a car to meet us at the foot of the hill, we found that the telephone had been cut off that morning because Percy had forgotten to pay the bill.

That was the first time I ever went to the house that was to be the home of my elder daughter, that I ever saw the grass-covered drying ground where coffee beans were once spread to dry on flagstones, the vault which is the hurricane shelter, the ruined chimney smothered in coralita. Beside the lawn at La Haut there is a long low wall with maidenhair fern in its cracks beyond which crotons, frangipani, hibiscus have a background of a blue sea. La Haut has more colour to break the shade of the saman trees than anywhere I know: scarlet of spathodea, yellow of cassia, purple of bougainvillea; begonias and orchids on the trunks of the trees; and, for three days of the year, an outbreak, a superlative blooming, of a yellow vine spread like a mantle over the topmost branches.

That was also the first time we ever saw the emerald drop, that startling flash of green caught for an instant on the horizon as the sun vanishes into the sea and the world turns grey. Minutes after, scarlet banners in the sky proclaimed the day's death, and tiny lights flickered where the town of Roseau stood on a sand spit at the river's mouth.

2 Dreaming the dream

Paul Ninas' dwelling place – where Holly was staying – was in the north of the island above the village of Calibishie. It was built in Samoan fashion and consisted of a conical sugar-trash roof set upon 16 posts, with one central pillar to support the rafters. On the circular cement floor stood six chairs, a table, a bed, and an easel on which was the portrait of two nude negroes, one wearing a bowler hat and the other a scarlet handkerchief bound about a halo of tight plaits. Elsewhere were boards and bundles of shingles, for Paul had intended to build a real house when he could afford it. Meanwhile, or presently as the West Indian says, when he means now, this woodpile had become the home of an almost tame agouti, a creature something between a rat and a rabbit, which is indigenous to Dominica, and hunted by men with dogs. Furtively she emerged at intervals to seize the pigeon peas and pieces of sweet potato spread on the floor for her delectation.

We came to this place for the first time at sunset, by a red clay path winding between rows of bay trees. There had been a three-hour journey in the coastal launch from Roseau to Dominica's second town, Portsmouth, where we waited two hours, and then a rugged hour and a half in the bus. Golden light lay on the sea and on the French islands to the north, Guadeloupe, Marie Galante and the Saints, while the north-east corner of Dominica was lost in purple shadow, with only here and there a distinctive tree standing out against sky or ocean. Outside Paul's house, called a *moulin* for its likeness to the local sugar mills, coarse grass and scrubby bushes stretched to the cliff's edge, below which pink-tipped waves covered flat coral for a width of quarter of a mile before resting on the strip of sand under coconut palms which is Calibishie beach.

Lennox and I took possession of the bed. Holly and his servants slept in his neighbour Clifford Nixon's house below the bay trees. There were two houseboys, Medly and Copperfield, the latter solemn, wall-eyed, and an assiduous reader of the Bible, marking his place in the Old Testament with a joker and that in the New with the ace of spades. Furthermore, he collected postage stamps in a small tin box which had contained lozenges because he had read somewhere that he would be given a gold watch for a hundred or a thousand or a million.

Medly was a cherubic lad, dark enough, but not toned to quite such boot-black consistency as Copperfield. He was younger, more simple, wearing brilliantly pink shirts and a felt hat. He even served dinner in a hat, and when remonstrated with on this score said he feared the night air, and was seen rubbing off his headgear against one of the posts before coming to the table, reminding one of a horse scratching its back on a fence. Holly, who had lived for so long in the South Seas, tried in the beginning to make his servants wear only a loincloth, the *pareu* of Tahiti. Friends had assured him that this was impossible, that West Indians would never agree; but when asked to do so Medly and Copperfield had consented immediately. "You see?" said Holly, "one has only to make the suggestion." Thus were the friends confounded until dinner-time, when the boys appeared wearing the red and white cotton *pareus* over all their other clothes in the form of a sash, looking like small boys playing pirates.

Every morning at breakfast Medly and Copperfield brought coalpots to the table and toasted bread over the charcoal, piece by piece as Holly directed, crouching as might witches round a cauldron, or priests making a burnt offering on some mysterious altar.

This was Holly's second winter in Dominica on account of which, and because he was interested in food, he took over the housekeeping. On fine mornings Lennox and I would disappear on to the red rocks or to a beach, and would return to find Holly swinging in a hammock clad only in a loin cloth.

"What is there for lunch?" we would ask, and the invariable reply would be, with a slight note of query as though he were proposing an innovation: "Why, I thought we would have a little salad." Inevitably, there would be more for lunch than salad but he loved to give the impression that he had sat there for the whole morning pondering how best to blend one tomato, a few string beans, and watercress.

If the weather were unpropitious, then we would watch the process of housekeeping, which went something like this.

"Good morning, Sir, Good morning, Madame. I bring you eggs."

"How many eggs?"

"I have four eggs, Sir. Two are for money and two are for you."

For two eggs we used to pay a penny-halfpenny. But the "two-are-for-you" constituted a present for which a return had to be made in kind, either a cigarette or a tot of rum from the demijohn, rum always taken neat with a chaser of water. It was a moot point whether it was more expensive to receive a present or to make a purchase.

"Good morning, Sir. Good morning, Madame. I bring you goat." Then Copperfield would be sent for.

"Is this young goat, Copperfield?"

And Copperfield would press and pinch the rather unsavoury looking piece of meat and say: "Not very old goat, Sir." Then the meat would be purchased at sixpence per pound, both sides guessing at the weight, which was generally decided in favour of the vendor.

When Copperfield acquired a piece of meat too good to be stewed on a coalpot then he would borrow, for threepence, the village oven where bread was baked, an oven plastered white, under a thatched roof; and as we came home at dusk our nostrils would be assailed by an infinitely succulent smell.

Or again we would hear: "Good morning, Sir. Good morning, Madame. I bring Madame a present." This would be a tight bunch of flowers, roses, tiny carnations, Michaelmas daisies, oleanders, with a spray of asparagus fern; and sometimes "roots" – yams or sweet potatoes, or cush-cush, which last is a kind of yam, mashing to a pretty shade of mauve.

Once we had a present of a piece of fish called "cong". This was identified as conger eel, and was looked at by Medly and Copperfield with the greatest scorn.

"Who sent the cong?" we asked the boy who brought it.

And were told: "Mr Saloo does not use cong, but he send it to you." Which sounded sinister.

We cooked a piece and gave it to the cat, a cat called Delicat, belonging to Copperfield's sister, and it neither died nor was sick. So we boiled the rest of the cong with a shilling in the saucepan, for it is said that if fish is bad it will turn silver black. The shilling came out bright and clean, so we ate the cong, and neither died nor were even sick, whereas Medly and Copperfield were impressed and astonished. Only we did not accept any more presents of that particular fish because we did not like it very much.

Gradually we evolved a way of life, a rhythm; and we began to break into component parts surroundings which seemed to us breathtakingly lovely, and which are still lovely in spite of all that man does in the interests of his daily bread to make them otherwise. One of the saddest things I ever heard said was by an Englishman who had been 20 years in

Dominica to whom we waxed lyrical about sea and river and mountain. "Why, yes," he said in a surprised way, "I remember when I first came to Dominica I thought it beautiful." How terrible to have forgotten appreciation, to be blind to all but the common task.

Before breakfast, when the sea was still pale, we would swim in the bay called 'Ti Baptiste, less musically known as Black Beach. We would push a way through Clifford's bay trees, cross red rocks powdered with tiny cacti and golden-backed ferns; and, by a series of steps made with a cutlass, climb down the cliff on to the sand which Copperfield insisted on calling blue, but which is in reality heavily black, black as coal but less dirtying. The beach is perhaps a hundred yards long, guarded by cliffs whose foliage has been blown almost horizontal by the prevailing wind. Atlantic rollers, deterred but not checked by a barren island, play with dead trees or a broken raft.

Before lunch, when the shadows of the coconut palms were short and squat and the seagrape and almond trees had almost no shadows at all, we would bathe in the bay called Grand Baptiste or White Beach, where the sand consisted of powdered shells and coral and was pink or white or biscuit-coloured according to the sun's shining. The waves were as large as those in 'Ti Baptiste, but the reef was more effective. A brown rock created a deep pool where we might spy shoals of bright blue fish, black fish with yellow stripes, red and orange and purple fish, and those little sepia ones which we call coney fish because they play in and out of holes like rabbits.

At tea-time, we bathed on Hodges beach, where the sand

Grand Baptiste bay, known as White Beach, close to the Napiers' home, Pointe Baptiste, in the north of Dominica.

is grey and strewn with logs and coconut husks and water-soaked almonds, fronting a pale yellow island honeycombed with horizontal blowholes. Here the river ran parallel to the sea, making a wide pool for muscovy ducks and slow lazy fish called dormi and brochet. We would swim first in the sea, and afterwards in the cold river. And then would walk home through the forest on narrow silent paths cut off from even the sound of the waves; or else by the high road which in those days was heaped with loose metal or broken coral, but which had always a little beaten track on it, worn smooth by the bare feet of the peasant people. These, as we passed, would say good night, or good evening, or good afternoon, but never the phrase that we expected, so that we remembered the Chinese game of "scissors, paper, string"; for if we said good evening they said good night, or vice versa.

Before dinner Holly would almost literally keep open house, for how could you close that which had no sides. Copperfield's uncle, bringing us a present of drinking coconuts, would sit half hidden by cane trash to play draughts with his nephew on the edge of the cement floor. Lucinda, who had once upon a time been the mistress in the *moulin*, would come to remove her cat who had been unjustly accused of stealing our butter; or the loony child of the village prostitute would creep around on the chance of picking up a cigarette tin or a "penny bread".

Clifford wanted help in building a still for the processing of bay leaves. In the botany book these were called *pimenta acris* and from the extract of their leaves there came eventually bay rum. Clifford's trees were slim and graceful, shedding their bark almost like eucalyptus trees, to reveal a polished surface, cream coloured or red. There was one still in the village already. One hundred pounds of leaves, Clifford told us, would yield one pound of oil, and one pound of oil would bring in three shillings of which the distiller took half. Clifford had the notion that if he built his own still he could keep the three shillings.

Bennett the fisherman dropped in to ask if we had any flour sacks because he wanted to make a new sail for his boat. It would take 12 sacks to make a sail. Early in the morning the little square-sailed fishing boats, most of them no more than dugout canoes, would put gaily to sea; and at dusk were drawn up under coconut palms. When fish had been caught, the fishermen blew conch shells and then everyone would gather with their pennies while the dorado or tuna were hacked to pieces with a cutlass.

One day there were smugglers in the tiny cove below the house. Early in the morning a stranger came up the cliff and asked us in French, in real French not in the French Creole patois of Dominica, if Mr Paul were there. And when I said Mr Paul was in America he ran away very quickly. No one, unless standing on the cliff right beside our privy, could have seen the boat which was of an altogether different cut from Dominican ones. Three men sat there all morning while the sun beat down on to the rocks, and waves slapped lazily against the shingle. Word went round the village: "The Frenchmen are here." And people borrowed money from us and from each other to buy tobacco and French wine. Towards midday we saw the boat crawl, heavily laden with coconuts, through the passage in the reef. All afternoon the little white sail could be seen tacking backwards and

View from Pointe Baptiste towards red rocks (above) and (right) nearby 'Ti Baptiste bay, known as Black Beach.

forwards until at dusk there was a faint light hardly to be distinguished from those luminous beetles called labelles.

Later, lying on the hard bed under the mosquito net, we listened to the giant crickets called crak-crak, and the shrill tiny ones that make a noise like a buzz saw. There would be a rustling of lizards in the thatch, and the labelles would whirl round and round each other in a mad dance, flashing themselves on and off like electric torches. Running on floor or wall they resembled motorcars with head and rear lights turned on, and by imprisoning three under a tumbler it was possible to see to read.

A pool filled with rainbow fishes; palm trees sprawling over white sand; a seascape shifting, dissolving, but always new. No wonder we dreamed the dream of ownership, played if and suppose, putting a house thus and a garden so. Lennox had always longed for Tahiti, to go back there to live. Now we saw possibility of an alternative.

Exactly when the idea took shape I do not remember. Perhaps it was always there, from the first morning when we went down on to the promontory on what we called the red rocks below the *moulin* where the rain had made deep water courses and the sea had scoured out caves. A narrow, precipitous path had been cut by fishermen from the scrub and foot holes carved in the rock face. Now and then a blade of razor grass would catch at our ankles, or a bush whip back to show resentment of our passing. The cliffs were brick red or ochre in a fierce sunlight under which ferns and cacti threw shadows as grotesque as though spiders had congealed beneath our feet. Out of a hole in the rocks, spray was blown upwards as from a spouting fountain.

From that place we looked across to the strip of white sand and seagrape trees of Grand Baptiste. Within a week we had plotted what we wanted, found out to whom the land belonged, made a tentative proposal to buy it, climbing bay trees to estimate the view, and beating possible boundaries with an old woman who called me Belle Madame, and who said that her grandfather having been a white man she understood the ways of white people.

Two generations before we came to Dominica, a Frenchman from Martinique had bequeathed that headland and two valleys to his descendants, *aux enfants des enfants des enfants, jusqu'à sept generations*. Roughly 16 people, so-called the company, were in the direct line of succession, holding the land in common with the right to make a garden, to graze a goat. A "garden" in the West Indies means essentially a provision ground; and on this poor soil only a patch of cassava or sweet potatoes would grow. A further complication was that the family was divided. Some members lived in Atkinson, on the edge of the Carib Reserve; one in Portsmouth; one in the north-east town of Marigot. One had even disappeared in Cayenne, where long ago people sought their fortunes, as more recently they did in Curaçao and the United Kingdom. Now and then, ancient gold coins or earrings from Guiana have been deposited with me against loans.

Residents of Calibishie were pleased to sell part of the company holding, not for the value of the purchase price –

we offered £100 for the site, approximating eight acres – but because they believed us to be the right kind of white people, that our presence in the village would lend prestige and promote the circulation of ready money.

Fifty shillings cash down, which was an advance on the purchase price, was of itself little compensation for the scratch crop of cassava, the tethering of the odd pig under a *poix doux* tree; although £12 per acre was, on the other hand, considered a fantastic price to pay for cliff and scrub and a few pockets of poor soil. We also paid heavy compensation for every potato, avocado and bay tree.

The outlying members of the family, however, could see no benefit whatever in the transaction. They said they did not want *buckras* (white people) in the village who might well interfere with the smuggling trade. How far they had legal right to spoil the bargain for brothers and cousins was never made clear. In any deal concerning land, as in family quarrels, there was always a long and complicated trail of unregistered title deeds and unproven wills. These contained such items as "To my sons Simeon and Clive my mare that her produce shall be divided equally among them." And, "to my daughter Jeanillia the services of the bull, whenever she shall require them."

There came a Sunday when we hired the mail bus and arranged to meet the Atkinson branch of the family in Marigot, taking with us for purposes of persuasion Stephen Laville, the grey-haired patriarch of the Calibishie branch. But the family defaulted, simply did not turn up. Whereupon we pursued them on foot, fording the Pagua river and following the harsh trail almost to the borders of the Carib Reserve, carrying the purchase money – in bullion – in a paper parcel.

I have mental snapshots of that day, as it might be stills of a too long film. One is of Stephen wriggling with embarrassment when, smitten with cold feet about being involved in selling the land, he was discovered most basely trying to slip off the back of the truck and into the church in nearby Wesley. And another, of two sulky men, interrupted in the building of a boat, glowering at their elder brother, who planned to sell for a mess of potage a birthright to land they never used nor wanted. And again I see myself sitting on a narrow couch in a two-roomed house whose walls were, as in most Dominican houses, pasted over with holy pictures and cigarette cards and cuttings from magazines, facing a chiffonier laden with odd pieces of china, and glasses in three colours. A brown woman, hastily retrieved from her garden by a copper-coloured man, said she had not kept the tryst in Marigot because she had a new baby. "Where is the baby?" I inquired politely. And was told: "Madame, behind you."

On a cushion, which I had thought to be merely one cushion among many, and which I had by the sheerest fraction not sat down upon, I now perceived black boot-button eyes in a coffee-coloured face that was strangely old and wise for its two weeks of existence. I often think that had I moved that fraction backwards and smothered the child how altogether different would the rest of my life have been.

We sealed the bargain in Marigot, that small town built on many hills in a forest of breadfruit trees, meeting in the house of Stephen's cousin, a lean pale man who welcomed us in pyjamas. He had not accompanied us to Atkinson on the plea that he was sick of a fever. And there, at three in the afternoon of a very hot day on which we had not lunched, he produced a bottle of warm beer which, hot or cold is an expensive drink in Dominica, opened it ceremoniously among 10 people and served it in liqueur glasses. And this the "company" sipped sacramentally to the success of the venture, while beyond the house the north-east trades blew over a wild and tempestuous sea.

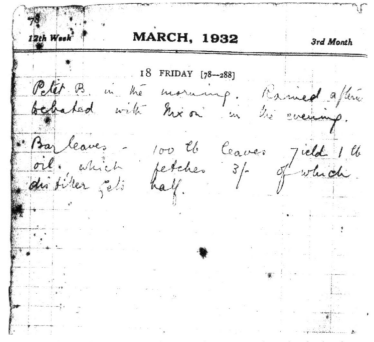

From Elma's diary: in March 1932 the Napiers bought the land at Pointe Baptiste, near the village of Calibishie.

It was many weeks before the purchase could be finally effected and only patience such as Lennox's could ever have unravelled the complications and brought the owners to a deed of sale. And when at last the night came for the vendors to sign the papers – hurricane lamps throwing shadows on to the trash roof of the *moulin*, smells of smoke and rum and tobacco, a grumbling of surf above the shrilling of frogs and crickets – it was found that the deed had been made out in the wrong names, in the names of the people as we had come to know them, Mon Brun, Ma De, and Tisson, but not in the names they came ceremoniously to put on paper. It transpired that most people had two names, the baptismal one plus surname or "title", which was used only on Sundays; and another haphazard one, a nickname, by which means the devil, powerless on the sabbath, might be cheated of his prey.

At long last, however, the deed was properly executed; the final instalment paid. We told the villagers we would come back "some day", perhaps even in two years. But on our return to London in March 1932, Lennox's cousin pointed out that if his heart was so fixed upon another place he would be of reduced value in the business. So we folded our tents and in November of the same year returned to Dominica, known at that time as the Cinderella of the Caribbean, the unlucky stepchild. With us were the children, Patricia, aged seven, and Michael, aged four, and my 20-year-old daughter Daphne.

3 | Of mud and cockroaches

We reached Dominica by the same French ship as we had arrived on our first visit. It had been induced to make a special call. On a night of clouded full moon, the roofs of Roseau glistened with intermittent rain. Mountains, bowed like Atlas, held back the sky from pressing the town into the sea. Boats swarmed about the gangway to take us ashore with our vast amounts of luggage. Two boats were lashed together to receive the car.

"*Regardez-moi donc ça,*" said the chief officer, "*c'est inouï.*" It's unheard of. He offered to take the Morris on to Martinique and there re-ship it, forgetting that when it returned to Roseau it would still have to be landed in the same way.

Inevitably, I had dressed the children too early. It seemed a century since we had left Guadeloupe – the flat-faced, grey-jalousied French houses, the glaring yellow dock, the pale water with a gleam of turquoise in it. Since midnight we had watched the land of our desire loom in blue-black immensity, had seen it draw nearer and nearer. So near, in fact, that we thought we must ram the cliff. As the anchor chain rattled we were looking down and into the town.

In wide, silent streets, water made shiny surfaces, and poured through open drains. We found our beds in Cherry Lodge, the boarding house, but no one slept. Cocks crowed and dogs barked. At five o'clock, the cathedral bell began ringing. At half-past six, a grey wet dawn, with fanfare of rain on tin roofs and spluttering of gutters, ushered in our new life.

For two days it rained almost without ceasing. Cold winds swept down the valley to meet the sea. The river ran angrily, putty coloured, threatening bridges and retaining walls. We crouched on the beds to play cards with the children. Percy found us so doing at nine o'clock on the first morning and straightway fell in love with Daphne – "From the first moment I saw her, playing rummy with Michael at Cherry Lodge." He had come to tell us that our temporary house at Calibishie, which he had promised to build for us in our absence, was by no means ready. I had intended to go there immediately, to the deep clear pools and sandy beaches of which we had talked all through the London summer. We had not expected to live with bored children in a rain-soaked town.

That afternoon we hired a car to go for a bathe in the Everton river, near Loubiere on the south coast. There we crossed an abandoned garden at the edge of a flooded stream. Giant leaves of dasheen poured out water as we shook them in passing. Mud clogged our feet, and the

Lennox and Elma with their children Michael and Patricia in Dominica, 1933

prickles of wild eggplant tore at the children's legs. Palms and cocoa trees, limes with tiny cacti powdering their branches, dripped in sombre melancholy. I had visualised Pat and Michael's delight in running water and the right to play with it. Here were peevish chilly children overcome by altogether too much water.

Next morning, we decided at all cost to move on, to camp once again in Paul's *moulin*, to compel by our presence speed among carpenters. There was no through road to our property so our car must come to the Northern district by sea. Towed by launch, it safely made the 20-mile or so journey, still resting on the same canoes. In those days, no one knew distances exactly. One measured by time: such and such was an hour's walk, somewhere else two hours by horse.

Our journey from Roseau to Portsmouth was by the public launch. First-class passengers, seven or eight a side, faced each other with knees touching as though to play up-

There was no road from Roseau to Dominica's second town, Portsmouth, so travel was by public launch.

Jenkins. That day drips from the roof fell with the regularity of a Chinese torture, while canvas curtains, when lowered against the rain, kept out the air. Along the coast, water poured through gullies, which were normally dry, falling over cliffs, spouting from every crevice. Where the clouds lifted, silver ribbons could be seen streaking the dark forest of the mountain tops. At every village, where grey houses huddled about the mouths of rivers, and fishing nets were spread to dry over seagrape and guava bushes, there was a clamour of passengers and pigs and fowls, with contentious transfer of baskets and sacks. People and freight together were flung into canoes already quarter filled with water in which floated fish scales or refuse of fruit. Dangerously, the little boats tossed to make their landing; men standing knee deep in the sea to bring them through the surf on to the shingle.

At Portsmouth there was an exasperating delay in unloading our gear. We were racing against time for in November it is dark at five-thirty. To convey us to Calibishie we had chartered the "bus", a vehicle whose body was tied together with string, and liable to part company with the engine at any corner. When heavily weighted at the back, the bus had been known to rear, the front wheels remaining off the ground until sufficient persons sat on the mudguards to restore balance. Carrying passengers, mail and mixed freight it gave a bi-weekly service as far as Marigot and back on an up-and-down track of hairpin bends that was little more than a ribbon of mud, coated with grey metal lightly spread.

The bus lumbered over the road, displacing stones, scattering puddles, carrying us over the divide of the island, down on to the Atlantic shore where, at Blenheim, a slow green estuary, winding under coconut palms and wild ginger, meets the sea among islands long since torn from the forbidding cliffs. Our seats were un-cushioned boards, the roof more in the nature of a lid than a shelter. Rain blew in from all sides. At the entrance to Hampstead House – a rutted grass track, windbreak of dark trees, sodden limes and grapefruit in a heap by the roadside – a white man and two children were waiting to greet us, but there was no time to stop and talk, no time before dark, no time. "We were a little hurt," the man said next day, "but afterwards we understood."

On the hill at the far side of Calibishie village a few old friends were waiting, but it was hard to recognise dark faces in the gloom and confusion. On the path to the *moulin* from the main road, water had collected, ankle deep, into red pools. Bare-footed women, seeing that the children made no progress, took these in their arms and forcibly carried them, they yelling with outraged dignity. In the grey dusk that makes for a few minutes of twilight, soaked, muddied, and utterly weary, we came into that single open-sided room into which wind was blowing. It seemed to be full of people

The Napiers' moulin - built to a traditional Arawak design - where they lived before Pointe Baptiste was built.

Elma in the moulin, and Patricia in fancy dress of dried leaves.

while hurricane lamps, dowsing the last of daylight, made a dim glow. Copperfield waited at our disposal. He said: "The agouti, it die. But it eat good."

There was the old double bed, the hammock, and two mattresses we had brought with us. The roof leaked, and dust from the sugar trash lay on the table. The nude negroes on the easel had been replaced by a self-portrait of Paul's, dark-haired and swarthy; and beside it stood Copperfield's attempted copy of the same, the face unnaturally white; this being, we could only suppose, the black man's most sincere form of flattery. Next morning, when we unpacked, we hung our clothes over both pictures. Lodging had been found for May and Sarah, whom we had re-employed on the principle of "better the devil we know", but within a few days they were complaining that there was "no basin; no utensil; no happy feeling." In Dominica the word utensil refers solely to a chamber pot.

Soon after dawn, partly for cleanliness' sake and partly so that Lennox might sleep longer, Daphne and I set out with the children to bathe at Grand Baptiste. It was still raining, but we said: "We'll go into the sea to keep dry." I had underestimated, however, or had forgotten the muddiness of the path, imagining perhaps that it had been part of a nightmare, a product of the dark. We slipped and slithered down a precipitous clearing where I remembered white orchids, dry scrunchy leaves, and a patterned sunlight. All summer I had been dreaming of a deep green pool in a blue ocean; in moments of fatigue and anxiety I had said to myself: "It'll be all right when we get there. There will be White Beach."

Now I found grey inhospitable waves into which one hardly dared venture. And as a last straw the vegetation had been cleared (in doing which Clifford had attacked a poisonous manchineel tree, some of the sap touching his eye and temporarily blinding him. "Give me back my sight," he had cried to the doctor. "I will pay you anything. I will pay you even £20.")

Thus our private bathing place had been exposed not only to prying eyes but to a bitter wind. The children, who had slid down the hill, had to be carried up it. We were all dirtier than before. Back at the *moulin* I threw myself on the bed, disillusioned and exhausted. "I brought you here to enjoy yourselves," I quoted defiantly from This Year of Grace, "and enjoy yourselves you shall." And then somebody offered Pat a "jelly" which she accepted with enthusiasm, visualising a carmine, floppy shape smothered in whipped cream that she had met with at London parties. Instead, she saw a man hack off with a cutlass the green outer husk of a coconut and having decapitated the inner fruit, pour into a jug what looked like dirty water with grey foreign bodies floating in it. Left in the immature nut was the soft white jelly-like substance, which can be extracted with spoon or finger. The child was heartsick with disappointment.

Seldom have I known weather to be so cruel or so cold. Tempestuous showers scudded from the east to blend their vapours with spray blown off gigantic rollers. The French islands were invisible, our own mountains lost in clouds. From cracks in the rocks we call red, but which can be purple under rain or yellow in sunshine, waterfalls poured on to the black sand and stained the sea orange. I had promised to show the children big lizards of the kind they call *abolo*, grey-black with a smear of blue on them, but these were hibernating, and who could blame them. "The ground lizard," says Thomas Atwood, who wrote A History of Dominica in 1792, "has lately been discovered to be an excellent remedy for the leprosy, when made into broth." Fortunately, leprosy was the least of our troubles.

A few weeks later, there was a letter from England saying: "It was so brave of you, when you found all that mud, not to come back." How could we go back? We had burned our boats.

We moved from Paul's *moulin* into the little building, which afterwards became our guesthouse, on November 18 1932, the 13th anniversary of my first meeting with Lennox in Honolulu. As I set foot on the veranda, the head carpenter chalked a ring around my feet and claimed that the house be christened in rum for all hands.

The house was made of native woods, the boards badly assorted but often beautiful. When wet, the shingled walls and roof took on the deep red appearance of old tiles. There were two bedrooms, eight feet by 12, and between them a dining-room opening on to a small veranda facing a distant view of Morne Grand Bois, which from this angle is shaped like the eye tooth of a dog. A bed and a camp cot were put into each room; while a fifth couch stood in a *moulin* which had been erected a hundred yards away in small imitation of Paul's, with the addition, on the weather side, of interlaced branches of coconuts. Lennox and I slept there on alternate nights; hearing under the beat of the sea, wind rustling the thatch, hermit crabs scraping on the concrete floor.

It served also as a general sitting room and store. Trunks and suitcases carried the incongruous labels of Hotel Adlon, Negresco Palace, Golden Arrow; while on other shelves, labels of another kind gave us our one touch of decoration. Mice and beetles played endless hide and seek among tins of tongues and peaches and salmon until cockroaches devoured their pictures, so the tins became anonymous. Then there was no colour any more in that room.

In front of the *moulin*, a patch of cassava was removed to make a lawn. Beyond it we had view of a cold grey sea and could watch, on the furthest point of rock, the periodical uprush of water from the blowhole. Sometimes, when there is very little wind, spray hangs on the air above it like breath on a frosty morning; and, very rarely, the sea will be so calm that it ceases altogether to blow.

Almost the first thing to be unpacked had been the gramophone. For hours on end Noel Coward's songs from Words and Music – "A Younger Generation", "The Party's Over Now", "Mad Dogs and Englishmen" – blared to an indifferent sea. It seemed incredible that only three weeks previously we had been sitting in the stalls of the Adelphi theatre in London watching that revue. And to this day those same tunes, or a snatch of words, will call up memories of straw and rain and packing cases, of mud which balled like snow on sandshoes and espadrilles, of cockroaches found half drowned in wash basins, and having to be finished off with a toothbrush. With an aching and altogether unreasonable nostalgia, I can still visualise my little son in his red bathing suit clutching a flea-ridden puppy; Holly, with stained fingers, chain-smoking Gold Flake cigarettes, and a friend, Peter Dewhurst, doodling four-room plans of a house he meant to build and never did. And I remember, too, the ground dove brought captive in a wooden cage as a present to the children, and fed by them on a golden fruit they called, all in one word, "birdsberries"; a dove as soon as possible released but, alas caught all over again and doubtless eaten, for these are foolish birds.

Within a few days we inadvertently became a house party. Holly had returned from a summer in the States, and was planning to make his winter home 15 minutes' walk away at Hodges. Peter was an Englishman who had found Dominica by a similar accident to ours and who also stayed forever, marrying a Dominican girl and having many children. Lorna came from Spain in a sailing ship and brought with her a Dutchman she had picked up on the voyage. All these camped in Paul's *moulin* or lodged in the village, sharing our meals until Holly established himself in his half-built house where he picnicked in a state of architectural turmoil concealing a certain incoherence of design under a professional affectation of method, measuring his labourers' day with a huge watch. "Time," he would shout at noon; and again at the end of the lunch hour, "Time," breaking off a conversation in mid-syllable.

Masons, carpenters and unspecified persons swarmed over our land in preparation for the building of our main house. Stone for the foundations was stacked outside the kitchen and smelt rather horribly of the sea. New paths were cut through the scrub, revealing unexpected views, and strange trees whose dark branches made an effect of caverns, carried a fruit like an unripe apple that was poisonous to fishes. Palm trees bore seeds like apricots, while a white-flowered *pois doux*, most conspicuously unlike a sweet pea, filled the air with a cloying scent. Somebody caught an iguana – it is said you can do this by whistling, slipping a noose around the creature while it is in a state of hypnosis – but, as in the case of the ground dove, we set free this edible lizard and it lived in our neighbourhood for a long time, its colour changing, chameleon fashion, with the branch whereon it rested.

The site itself was cleared of its bay trees and levelled. The Irish doctor, who visited the village clinic once a fortnight, mistook this with pleasure and subsequent disappointment for a hard tennis court. Lorna, thin and rather bitter in blue trousers, accused Lennox of trying to make Versailles in Calibishie. Everyone's nerves were a little strained and tense.

One night before dinner I was putting Pat and Michael to bed. Music drifted to us from the *moulin* syncopated by the sound of the waves. Where the trash kitchen stood, there was a fitful glow from a coalpot shining through coconut branches. Then Daphne came to me in a great rage, saying that Lorna claimed Beatrice Lillie's recording of "Mad Dogs and Englishmen" to be better than the author's own. "If that woman stays, I go," she said. Having soothed my daughter as best I might, I found a strange dog standing on the dining-room table preparing to eat the butter. "*Marche*," I shouted, which is the island way of execrating a dog, "*Marche*, you brute, get out." Pat called, "What is it, Mummy?" And when I had explained, she said with disappointment, "Oh, I thought it was Daphne shouting at Lorna."

Eleven years later, I happened to be crossing Venezuela by air with Noel Coward when we went all British together, vainly seeking a nice-cuppa-tea in glary airports where walnutty soldiers in olive uniforms examined our passports and Pan American hostesses invited us to Coca-Colas "on the house". And by way of conversation I related the saga of our early days in Dominica when his Words and Music had been part of our daily lives, and Daphne and Lorna had quarrelled about "Mad Dogs". "Your daughter was so right," he said. "I could not agree with her more." And then he told me the story that Winston Churchill and President Roosevelt had so violently disagreed about the wording of that same song that the Atlantic Charter of 1941 very nearly failed to be signed.

In that terrible beginning it rained for three weeks. But at last there came an evening of blessed sunshine, when the white town on Marie Galante quivered on the sea line, and the sky was eggshell blue above Morne aux Diables. Daphne and I went over to the point beyond the blowhole and looked across the tumbling water to our own land, seeing midget figures moving around the *moulin* and upon the house site. Spray fell on us like rain from surging billows tossing their foam into the air, spilling themselves against rocks from which they fell back to mingle with crashing, unswimmable surf. We thought how peaceful was this place, far from guests and children, from carpenters and masons and domestic servants.

Sarah was never a good cook, even making allowance for the discomfort of her kitchen. The last straw was a chocolate cake made for a picnic. "The baking powder," she said, "it run away with me." She had brought to Calibishie, not the spindle-legged boy who had shared her bed in the barracks, but a girl child; and soon we were finding that either the cook or the child was constantly indisposed, so that we began to see very little of Sarah. One night she disappeared altogether, hibernating for two days in the house of Giraud Nixon whose dwelling was one of the prettiest in the village, red painted and half lost behind yellow alamanda and an arch of crimson bougainvillea. When Giraud gave a dance – music with shakshak and boomboom and triangle; old-fashioned square dances in the nature of quadrilles – Sarah ran out at two o'clock in the morning into the midst of the party telling everyone to go home, which they most surprisingly did. But such behaviour did not make for popularity in the village, and we knew that the time had come for us to part.

We were satisfied that May, although so young, should be promoted to the position of cook. Culinary proficiency was in her ancestry. Then she ventured: "I have a sister by my mother's side who would like the place." Thus Louisa came from Roseau into our lives, quintessence – in appearance at any rate – of a stage parlourmaid trained in the best houses who, a few days after making her first entrance, directed on to the beach a Methodist minister who had come unexpectedly to call. Four Napiers, sunbathing in the nude, were eventually made aware of his presence by a series of discreet coughs.

May used to scrub the floors with half of a sour orange, and clean pots and pans with the heavy black sand from the beach at 'Ti Baptiste. On our first Good Friday she told us that an egg laid on that day would, if broken into a glass of water, set into a picture representing the future. ("They told

"George King, our yard man, whose duties were to carry water and burst wood, was wizened and ancient."

her how, upon St Agnes' Eve, young virgins might have visions of delight.")

George King, our yard man, whose duties were to carry water and burst wood, was wizened and ancient. Clifford introduced him as: "A foreigner to the island but it speaks English." A Barbadian by birth he wore trousers made, in a popular local fashion, to wrap over, dispensing with fly buttons; and was so small that he could have hidden easily in either leg. He was a useful servant until the demon drink defeated him; one of those, formerly found in all countries, who express their loyalty by referring to the family as "we" and to the family's possessions as "my". ("I go to feed my donkeys". "I rubbing my silver.") He was satisfied with five shillings a week, his midday meal, and the potato parings for his hog.

At first we fed the female servants altogether, thinking arrogantly that we would train them to a balanced diet and to cut down on starch. But very soon they complained that they did not like our food, and asked to be given two shillings extra wages instead, which was the custom of the country. Doubtless they had friends to dig and plant their vegetables, to give them fish. One day there was meat soup left over from our own meal. "Oh, no, Madame," Louisa said sternly, "we not using soup." And I was reminded of my sister's Scottish servants, lent to me in London in a moment of crisis, when it so happened that there were several pheasants in the larder. "Oh, no, Madam," said the parlour maid, "we do not eat bird."

Here there were customs and taboos about eggs, about eating a ripe banana in the heat of the day, about milk. "If

Stephen Laville, storekeeper and publican of Calibishie village, with Michael.

you not watering the milk in the bottle the cow will go dry, dry, dry." Once I offered Louisa the half of a custard pudding for her child. "But, Madame," she said, "I could not let him use egg," in a tone of voice as though I had offered arsenic. And when I protested to May about bringing up her child on arrowroot pap only, she said she could not be sure that he would always have the milk of the same cow, and so gave him none. Holly, to the day of his death, insisted on Medly eating "our" food – red meat and green vegetables – but he was no healthier or happier and possibly less so than those who consumed bowlfuls of purple dasheen or cooked green figs (bananas), which when skinned look like sickly sausages. If available a little fresh or salt fish would be thrown in as a "relish". ("Are the people hungry?" a visiting governor asked a country schoolmaster during the war. "Oh, not to say hungry, Sir. Only they have no food." Root vegetables are provisions, and only the relish rates as food.) When fridges came into use servants would not open them without putting on hat and coat.

Ambrosine, wearing spectacles with an air of ultra refinement, was the daughter of Stephen Laville from whom we had bought the largest portion of our estate. She was introduced by her father to look after our children, they being, however, quite incapable of submitting to discipline from someone so alien. Ambrosine had a house of her own, a grey wooden shack set among palm trees and roses, built on the land of her father who was village publican and storekeeper. Although Stephen could speak little English, an astonishing friendship was established between himself and Michael who, from a very early age, would slip down to the rum shop and play draughts with perfect strangers, returning almost invariably with some gift – a breadfruit, a piece of salt fish, a kitten.

It was Stephen who presented the children with the mongrel puppy known as Little Dog, who acquired great personality in the family. She brought us fleas and ticks and all the accompanying worries and heartaches that go with dog loving. There were small, brown active ticks, and elephant-grey sluggish ones full of blood, which varied in size with the amount taken. We removed these by hand and drowned them in tumblers; but I also witnessed mass migrations from Little Dog's body, pinhead-sized ticks climbing the wall behind my bed like a flight out of Egypt. We never found a more satisfactory name for her, although many were tried. So Little Dog it remained, preferable, obviously, to Little Bitch. Affection could be emphasised by stressing the Little, outrage by shouting Dog.

As she grew up, her barking so grated on Lennox, who had not been brought up with dogs and never really liked them, that we gave her away to a man in Marigot. Weeks later she found her way back to us, running the whole 10 miles to creep under my bed and thump her tail. So I said that never, never, would I part with her again, and never did until she died. (The obituary I wrote for the Manchester Guardian under the heading "A Dog is Dead" was reprinted in Synopsis and in the Animal Magazine, so that if immortality be the span of memory then Little Dog is still immortal.)

Ambrosine gathered clay from the red rocks which she moulded into semblance of animals, and made fancy dresses

A DOG IS DEAD

DOMINICA, B.W.I.

In the night the wailing of the puppies is like the crying of sea-birds, louder to my ears than the beat of the waves and more piercing than the shrilling of insects. Scrabbling, scrambling, in a blind world bounded by the four sides of a kerosene box, knocking their blunt pink noses against unknown substances, catching their claws in the woollen meshes of an old bathing-suit that is their blanket, they cry their hunger to an empty darkness. I light the stove, nursing the blue flame, warm milk in a saucepan, and pour it into a medicine bottle fitted with a teat; then, one after the other, pick the little cold creatures from their helpless fumbling and still their wailing with sustenance. Already they know the smell of warm rubber as twenty-four hours ago they knew their mother. Pink mouths open to show square tongues; round heads are pressed back upon my own breast;

Elma Napier wrote many articles for the Manchester Guardian about her life in Dominica, including this obituary for a much-loved dog.

for the children out of the huge leaves of the tree called *rosinier*, two leaves for a skirt and one for a hat, crowning the latter with flowers from her stepmother's garden, little tight wreathes of roses and big garlands of plumbago and hibiscus. But soon she became bored with us, or the children were too naughty. She told Percy, whether by way of information or invitation I do not know, that she must have a man every fortnight, else she was ill; and, after staying away on account of a cold, she decided to call our place well lost for love, and departed for the big city. "Madame, I will tell you the truth," King said, and proceeded to do so with some gusto. "She would have liked you to speak crossly to her; but, Madame, no one can find fault with your ways."

This was gratifying, but left us without a children's maid. (How odd to remember that servants were once taken for granted. As in England these have been absorbed by the shop and the factory, so here there is the lure of the "field", of the task work that may be finished by noon.)

One night I asked Louisa to sit with Pat and Michael in the *moulin* through our dinner hour; and then May came to me, tense with her displeasure, saying: "Louisa has pressed." We stared at her blankly, not yet having understood that if a woman has been ironing clothes she cannot be exposed to the damp air, but should sit all evening in a closed room; as when a relative has died, and windows are shut lest the spirit of the dead enter. Neither should she cross water; nor press after washing dishes. Years later this same Louisa, always a friend and almost always obliging, refused point blank to iron a dress for me when I was summoned hastily to town, for the reason that she had just done the washing up. I was living then within five miles of Roseau so I told her to put an iron on the stove, ran down to swim in the cold river, and then pressed the dress myself, triumphantly exhibiting no evil effect whatever. "Madame is English," Louisa said. "It is different for we people."

In those days, Dominicans would not swim in a river before eleven in the morning, nor after five in the evening; nor go out in the rain, nor in the night air, without a hat. (There was the tale of the high court judge who, when the gentlemen were offered the Government House garden in which to relieve themselves after a dinner party, was seen to knot his handkerchief at the four corners to make a head covering.) Neither was it right to drink rum if one had been chewing cane, "for rum and cane together make colic sick".

In the market place there were complicated rules about "luck". If a woman's luck were "man" for instance, she must sell her first fruit to a person of the male sex, or to a female whose first child was male. Else would the fruit poison or the food perish. Thus do all peoples contrive to make their lives tortuous. A few years ago when I was complaining to a French cousin about the intolerable conventions which had restricted my life as a girl, he said: "Existence in those days was so easy for the rich that they had to invent something to make it complicated." The life of a West Indian peasant was never easy but his imagination made it harder. Or perhaps in some cases by simple faith, easier.

One morning a woman came to Lennox saying that Little Dog had attacked her, bruising her leg. And, refusing all medicament, she requested one of the dog's hairs to put on the sore place – asked quite literally for a hair of the dog that bit her.

◩

My husband's first task had been to prepare a vegetable garden: to have scrub felled and stumps extracted. The soil was poor and exhausted, our predecessors having gathered their crops and passed on, leaving coarse grasses tangled with convolvulus vines. We secured a gardener by the name of Cozier, an English-speaking Methodist, very tall, very opinionated, reputed to know something about the growing of English vegetables. Almost hourly he quoted his former employer, "Allport deceased", like a nanny or a governess boring her present charges with the virtues of the previous ones. Owing to some accident or deformity his toes were distressingly superimposed one upon the other.

Cozier's favourite expression was humbug. He would say of caterpillars, grinding their mashed bodies into the ground with his poor feet, "They humbug my fruit." Or again, before thinning the seedlings: "They humbug each other." Here, more than in most places, it seemed necessary to cross the fingers, to touch wood. Cozier would say: "If God spare, I will prepare mould for the tomatoes on Monday." He it was who showed us our first hummingbird's nest, a bowl of cotton the size of an eggcup, decorated externally with grey moss.

Stranger even than hummingbirds were those black and yellow caterpillars, six inches long and thick as my thumb, which preyed exclusively on alamanda and frangipani by munching with a pink mouth at one end and waving a small black tail at the other. In my bedroom I have found, laboriously moving across the floor, a white, turtle-shaped creature of microscopic dimensions, a scale insect, and a parasite on hibiscus. The garden book told us: "These can be kept in check by solutions of tobacco water or kerosene emulsions, which close up the breathing pores on the bodies of insects, cutting off their air supplies and suffocating them." And I thought, what brutalities one permits oneself: mashing the caterpillars or bisecting them with scissors, or pouring kettles of boiling water on to the nests of stinging ants. Where these, or termites, are concerned, the milk of human kindness is altogether dried up.

Just a few months after our arrival, our garden was

Michael and Patricia on White Beach – where the sand was "pink or white or biscuit-coloured according to the sun's shining".

lavishly yielding produce as it has never done since. We no longer needed to eat superfluous radish and turnip seedlings in order to provide ourselves with greens. Eventually Lennox, who was painstaking and always had green fingers, brought even green peas and asparagus to the table.

In those days there was extensive manuring and, during the *carême* or dry season, expensive watering. Before the tank under the veranda of the main house was built, girls and boys carried from the muddy stream that lay in the valley behind us, pails and kerosene tins on their heads, always with a few wide leaves floating on the water to prevent splashing.

At the sea's edge, amid refuse of conch shells and broken

coral and the purple poisonous jellyfish called Portuguese man-of-war, there was a sea moss which, boiled and flavoured with lime juice, would set into a jelly and become a prized delicacy, as were also sea eggs, which are the substance of the white sea urchins. The children and I brought up seaweed from Black Beach, remembering the kelp strewn on Scottish fields, the gulls and the curlew following the plough; but this well-intentioned effort was treated with scorn by our dependents. "That may be so in Scotland, Madame, but not in Dominica." Caribs, so I have been told, would not use manure at all, thinking the practice disgusting.

We had already bought a donkey for no other purpose. Mother Donkey in due course produced Robert (christened Robert-the-Bruce by Looby, our yard man, to whom I had lent a history book), the dearest, most intelligent, most affectionate donkey that ever substituted for a mowing machine; cropping the good grass, leaving the weeds.

(My own fingers are so conspicuously not green that even people I employ fail to make anything grow. So now, in my widowhood, I find myself among those whose rabbits practise birth control, whose goat strangles itself, whose pig, with Mrs Jack Sprat in mind, runs inordinately to fat.)

From the very beginning, we were initiated into the rhythm of planting by the moon. A pale crescent sinking into the dusk behind mountains affected one type of vegetable; an orange disc, bursting out of the sea at midnight, another. No sawyer would cut wood during the first or second quarters while the sap was rising, for the timber would soon rot and be attacked by borers. It has even been suggested that were an animal to be castrated in the wrong phase it would in consequence grow either long in body or thick in flesh. Plants intended to develop above the surface should be sown under a waxing moon, but root vegetables in the dark. Cabbages, however, might be planted three days before or three days after the full moon, which perhaps accounted for Cozier's preference for that vegetable, which he cultivated in absurd profusion and cherished exceedingly. (Boswell, in his journal for 1773, refers to the people of the Hebrides not choosing to cut peat at the increase of the moon.)

It was late in our first summer that Cozier was found gazing at the turned earth in the attitude of Rodin's *Penseur*. "Can you tell me," he said, "why this garden did better in the beginning when the soil was bad, than now when it has been made good?"

It had been for some time in our minds that results were incommensurate with expenditure. Freddie Warrington, in his little yard by the baker's, was doing far better than we with tomatoes, which we bought from him for our own use. We were young to Dominica, ignorant of her tricks, her obstinacies. Tomatoes only do well in new ground. The first crop is abundant, and afterwards they fail, are blighted, poison their own soil. I have seen it happen over and over. But Cozier said: "Clifford and I know that a spell has been put upon the land."

Clifford had come to borrow 30 pieces of silver with which to get married. This was the recognised fee for the priest, and it appeared that threepenny bits would do. He said he had not spoken to us about the garden but only to

Giraud Nixon, neighbour and prominent villager in Calibishie, with Patricia, and Michael on Giraud's pig.

Cozier – "because, boss, white people will not believe the things that black people know to be true." Clifford's grandfather had emigrated from the far west of Scotland, which had not caused his descendants to be any less superstitious. I remember him planting honeysuckle and hibiscus cuttings in a little flower garden he made for me, singing a runic charm; "This one cannot die. This will surely live." Now he had three explanations of our tomato trouble. One, that Cozier himself was secretly ill-using the garden, a malice so obviously to his disinterest that we did not consider it. Alternatively that someone was coming at dead of night cruelly to molest our seedlings. Clifford himself believed in the third possibility, obeah, the folk magic of the Caribbean.

We debated, tongue in cheek, who could have motive to

do us ill. It might be someone jealous of Cozier, wanting his job, which pointed straight at Freddie who had quarrelled with Cozier, drawing down upon himself the epithets viper and scorpion, and who was successfully growing tomatoes under his very nose. (This was the same Freddie who later replaced Cozier; in whose arms the old man almost literally died, who arranged his wake and funeral. Quarrels come and go in the West Indies, shift and change as elsewhere. New patterns of friendship form and dissolve.)

Within a few days Cozier sent to Portsmouth for some asafoetida which he mixed with kerosene and some other ingredient of which he would not tell us the name. These were to be burned and the ashes spread, but whether to prevent further spells or to reveal the perpetrator was not made clear. The tomatoes wilted as before and suspicion hung like a miasma over the village, while the enemies of Cozier blamed and were blamed.

King said: "It is not obeah exactly, but there is no doubt that these people can put spells upon the land to bind it." ("Exactly" was King's favourite word, as humbug was Cozier's. "Have you cleaned the gutters, King?" "Well, not exactly, Madame." "Have you bought fish?" "Well, not exactly.") The priest from Lasoye, which is the French name for the village of Wesley, pointed out that the sun was too hot in the autumn – September and October are our hottest months – for any but native vegetables to survive. Tomatoes are temperamental. Freddie's were flourishing in virgin soil. The coloured road engineer, coming to tea during the crisis, put forward the suggestion that when land is cleared it bears well. Then the roots of the felled timber begin to poison it.

4 | Building Pointe Baptiste

Within a month of our arrival in Dominica in November 1932, we had decided on the final plan of the house. In London, that previous summer, Lennox had sat up nights making designs for our house on paper showing a neatness and precision that were almost incredible in one not trained. His mansion – which we called Pointe Baptiste – was to be no trash *moulin*.

The large living-room of Pointe Baptiste faces west and north; a double bedroom fills the centre of the building; the children's two rooms are on the east, the veranda at that end being enclosed to make a playroom. The veranda fronting the sea is eight feet wide and 70 feet long, with an alcove that is in itself a sitting-room. We had to be very insistent about that feature for what West Indians call galleries tend to be skimpy or non-existent. Old estate houses in Dominica were not built for comfort nor for beauty being little more than adequate coverings for managers of absentee landlords, and sited to overlook the "works", the lime or cane-crushing machinery and the giant water wheel, rather than sea or mountain.

Our western windows look to Morne Diablotin, the mountain we had first seen from Sylvania, at nearly 5000ft the highest peak in the Lesser Antilles, and not to be confused with Morne aux Diables, a slightly lower peak in the extreme north. Morne is the French West Indian word for mountain, used alternately with *piton* – "highest peak" or "pointed summit". For *morne*, my dictionary gives "sad and gloomy" as well as "hill", and I wondered whether the early French settlers who bequeathed language and place names to these islands found the dark and impenetrable mountains depressing, longing for vineyards and wine-red clover, for the little pine trees of the Landes, or slow-moving rivers. Morne Diablotin, a mountain of many moods, may for days brood sullenly under a canopy of cloud and then will startlingly, often after a storm, stand out purple-black against the sunset, water pouring through gullies or over precipices; or may face the dawn, pink tipped, in perfect purity of outline.

Dominica was, in the 1930s, so hurricane conscious that to everyone but ourselves safety in time of storm seemed to be the only consideration, far more important than beauty of design or breadth of view. Our site was too near the cliff to please our few neighbours.

"Why not build in the windbreak?" they said. "You can make a path to the view, and place a seat at the end of it."

For the outbuildings – a kitchen and servants' house to be erected by the village carpenter – heavy timbers were felled high up on the mountainside where big forest was still standing within easy reach. When these had been roughly prepared they were brought down to us, eight men carrying each one and singing as they came, one man chanting a solo and the others chiming in with the refrain. All the way up the ridge path there were marks on the ground where the logs had been dragged. For days, even weeks, we listened to the click of wood on wood as shingles were examined, approved, rejected; shingles cut from the living heart of the tree at the right time of the moon.

The framework of the main house, however, was cut and prepared in Roseau from imported pitch pine, brought round to the north of the island by sloop and then erected by Roseau carpenters who thereafter took charge of operations. They made their mark in the village, spreading a little technical knowledge and leaving here and there a legacy to be recognised years afterwards by the name of a child.

I remember how anxiously we awaited our first boatload of pine, scanning the straits between Point Jaquet and the Saints. At dusk there was still no sign, and again at dawn we could see nothing but a pale pink ocean. But in a few minutes we heard the warning note of a conch shell and realised that the vessel was already tacking to anchor off Calibishie. There was never any landing stage there, and the entrance through the reef was narrow and marked only by stakes.

And so our house – in the form of timbers mortised and ready for erection, boards tongued and grooved – was transferred into little boats which were then rowed round the blowhole point to Black Beach. At the last moment the

Pointe Baptiste takes shape. The foundations were of coral, while the timber for the frame was landed on Black Beach in small boats.

boatmen demanded 50 shillings for the job, which to us did not appear unreasonable. But Clifford, acting as our overseer, became very passionate. "I think the people of this parish," he said, "are the wickedest people in all the world." And they retorted by calling him *philosophe*, which means busybody and is a great insult. It was Holly who afterwards propounded that this word must have been incorporated into the language of Dominica at the time of the French encyclopaedists when to be a philosopher was to be against the establishment. With the next consignment, our house was deliberately thrown overboard from the sloop and allowed to float on to the beach.

The foundations, high off the ground with space for bathroom and storeroom between them, were built of stone. Women in short faded dresses, men in trousers so patched that it was hard to trace the original garment, made endless procession, carrying water and sand for the mixing of mortar. White lime was made for us out of stacked coral, covered on top and on all sides with logs and branches which were kept slowly burning for two days, until the coral was reduced to a fine powder.

A West African statue embellished the top of the veranda steps at Pointe Baptiste.

One afternoon the bus bringing barrels of cement from Portsmouth overturned. Sand carriers, gardeners, water bearers, all sunk in somnolent three-o'clock-of-a-hot-afternoon attitudes, were galvanized into action by the arrival of a small boy with the news. Everybody rushed screaming to the rescue. Hampered by a blistered heel I arrived at the scene of the disaster just as the bus had been set on its wheels again. "That is nothing," said the driver, "just nothing at all."

Two days later, the first foundation was actually laid. Clifford told us it was customary to pour "hot" into the hole before the first stone was set. "All right," Lennox said casually, "you can ask the cook". Then Clifford had to explain that it was not hot water he wanted but a christening ceremony, consisting of a tot of rum to the masons. And a little rum was sacrificially poured into the hole before the drinks were served.

When the first of the kitchen timbers was erected this also had to be christened with rum as, a few days later, was the framework of the main house which, with its giant bones outstretched against the sky, looked like some colossal skeleton. With the first rafters a flag was hoisted consisting of a red *pareu*, the carpenters adding a bunch of hibiscus and an empty whisky bottle tied to a long pole.

Early in our building operations we had discovered what amounted to a spring of drinking water. A steep and narrow valley choked with tree ferns and *balisier*, a wild heliconia, was opened up to reveal a little bay known as Trou St Louis where there was a cave lined with tiny ferns, and giant roots of trees twisted into coils as though pythons had made anchorage, and where water dripped from the overhanging cliff. We were told that a fugitive from justice, presumably called St Louis, had been hidden in this *trou* for a month until friends took him away by night to the French country. Whether this happened 20 years ago, or 50, or 200 we never discovered. They said, "It is one long little time."

Pails were put under the three strongest drips to ascertain what would be the yield of water, water filtered through 50 feet of solid rock. And when this was decided to be fully adequate a little tank was built in the cave – it must have been cold working down there, for the cliffs shut out the sun and the re-echoing sound of the waves is long and grim – and ever since, rain or fine, there have always been 18 inches of water, no more and no less, in the tank. And every morning, the yard man would bring up a kerosene tin full of the clear liquid which the servants would not drink because they say it tastes of the sea.

Pat and Michael learned to dive in the rock pool on this new beach. Red sea anemones hung like lumps of raw meat under grey boulders, and microscopic crabs, hiding in a flat slab of coral, put out a tiny claw to nip anyone rash enough to sit down. Each lazy surge of the sea filled the pool with sky-blue fish, while overhead there was a white cedar which, losing its leaves in April, put out pink flowers to make one think of apple blossoms; and when these in their turn fell, they floated seaward like parachutes, spiralling on to the crests of waves.

For a brief period building went very quickly. Down in the *moulin* the gramophone was still playing:

I've had my fun
All that is done,
Why should I wish for more?
There's a younger generation
Knock, knock, knocking at the door.

Standing in the shell of the house amid swirling sawdust, with the hammers knock, knock, knocking at the roof, we tried mentally to place our chattels. Then everything hung fire interminably while window and door frames, hurricane shutters, cupboards and veranda rails were made. The worst period of all was the painting when, apart from the applying of four coats, every knothole, every crevice, had to be carefully puttied against the nesting of ants and cockroaches. We had decided on a pale yellow paint for walls and ceilings and had great difficulty procuring the right shade from Roseau. Samples came in the most peculiar colours, ranging from green to pink. Then someone remembered the word primrose. "Oh," they said, "Primrose? If you had told us you wanted primrose we should have understood. There is no yellow in primrose."

On pay day everyone would assemble at four o'clock and be called in turn – Soso George, Tisson Joseph, Virginia

Lennox Napier at
Pointe Baptiste, built
to his design.

Drygo – each to receive their money and a cigarette or a tot of rum. Clifford, waiting behind after the others would – as overseer – have both. In those days a "strong man" earned one-and-threepence a day, a less strong man a shilling, a woman seven pence, a weak woman sixpence. I do not know who assessed their calibre.

The most tiresome thing about paying was that no one ever had any change. There must be exactly the right sum for each wage. When funds were low a heavy parcel of coins would be sent from Roseau by courtesy of the launch mechanic and the bus driver. It might have been supposed that the silver distributed would have reassembled somewhere, but not even the rum shop could ever change a five-dollar bill, which in those days was the smallest note issued, equalling one pound and 10 pence, the island dollar being linked to sterling and British coinage used. The banks, of which there was none nearer than Roseau, kept their accounts in dollars and cents – but all tradesmen quoted prices in pounds shillings and pence. One day Holly stood in front of the cashier's cage at the bank together with a little old white lady who said: "You go first Mr Knapp. Mine is such a little cheque."

In April our furniture arrived, having been shipped direct from London, England to Portsmouth, Dominica. In spite of explicit instructions that cases should be small owing to lack of handling gear, one package weighed 45 hundredweight. How this was ever manoeuvred off the ship, on to the jetty and into the bus I cannot imagine. Many items had to be taken out before they could be handled at all, and these rested for a few days in the main street of the town, exposed to wind and weather.

Next day Ambrosine's father wrote or had written for him: "Sir, I am asking you kindly, if you are not in need of that box you brought in yesterday, please to sell it for me. Don't displease yourself if you require it, but if not please to grant me a favour, that I may make a private room in my shop, for it is small. Respectable yours."

Eventually he bought the case for 45 shillings, a price agreed upon in village conclave. And he did make a room of it, putting on a sloping shingled roof, and he and his wife slept there beside the stagnant river at the east end of Calibishie. Which was a sad thing to do, for his house on the hill, open to every breeze that blew, had as pretty a garden and as fine a view as any I know, whereas down by the river everybody was liable to fever.

The bus, laden with our possessions, arrived in Calibishie one late afternoon. Then persons of all sorts and sizes and kinds swarmed over and into the cases like bees entering hives, re-emerging with our household goods which we had last seen packed into vans on a grey London day, with the rain drifting down Mulberry Walk, and the wind blowing through an empty house. Now there was soft sunshine to greet them, and the sound of a lazy sea.

At last there came a Sunday, with the furniture all in place and Daphne and I enveloped in curtain materials, when we were taken aback by the entrance of hordes of people from Portsmouth who had come by the bus load, sightseeing. To this day I do not know who they were, having been far too embarrassed to register their features. They strolled through the house saying: "Ah", and "Oh", until we felt as might

The local passenger bus travelled between Portsmouth and Marigot. It carried the Napiers' furniture to Pointe Baptiste.

the owners of Knole or Chatsworth caught on a show day. I doubt if anyone much appreciated our primrose walls and rather cubist curtains, our violently tropical screen by Boulestin, and Nigerian masks and Fijian head rests. The Encyclopedia Britannica in its special case appeared to be more impressive than a whole wall of other books.

A few days previously there had been callers from Vieille Case, that far-away village we could see on the slopes of Morne aux Diables beyond Blenheim Bay. They drove behind a horse in a vehicle reminiscent of an Australian buggy and, having dismounted, surveyed the house lengthily with the air of practised architectural critics. Eventually we asked them to sit down, nervous for our chairs for the couple must have weighed 500lb between them. Over rum and cigarettes we found the conversation even heavier, they asking us playfully to guess how many children they had, and immediately supplying the answer which was 19. Duly impressed, I inquired of Madame how old was the eldest and was told 50, but upon my expressing surprise it transpired that she thought I had asked for her own age. Not for many minutes did they come to the point of the interview, which was a request for financial assistance. "My father is white," he said, "and her father is white, we do not cry our misery to black people."

Monsieur was as dark as they come in Dominica; Madame of a pretty café-au-lait colour, wearing a white silk dress, her enormous legs encased in white cotton stockings. There was a tale of a shop for which the license must be renewed, of bad debts, of a sloop sunk with 50 pounds worth of goods; a tale to make the heart bleed had we not heard it so often, and by now with many grains of salt. Begging from strangers was, in the days of Dominica's poverty, almost a national industry and no means confined to the destitute. Shamefacedly we explained – it was always we who were ashamed – that we had made a rule not to lend except to our own people in Calibishie. There was money enough out at grass in our own neighbourhood. "But," Monsieur said naively, "We did not talk of lending."

In those days, newcomers were inundated with begging letters; with requests for five shillings, one pound and £500. It was more embarrassing to refuse the former than the latter. Inevitably, when negotiating a loan, there was promise to cut a board, to make syrup; to reap a crop or sell a cow. Jewellery was deposited, or title deeds. Thus small debts accumulated which sometimes there was no intention of paying and which sometimes could never be paid. "I am asking you a favour. I get in trouble. I was playing dominoes and the police report me. I go to court. The court charge me £2. I don't have the money to pay." And from a total stranger, "An unexpected affliction in business obliges me to solicit your assistance to the extent of £15."

I spent the first day in the new house in bed. That was something I had been promising myself for six months and at last I had it.

The sense of space was almost frightening. Walls soared to misty heights, and between dressing-table and wash basin there stretched limitless plains. The sea was nearer, louder; and from the back windows I could see, as I lay prostrate, strange trees waving, different trees, while the square of sky beyond the veranda was altogether new.

When the drive was completed, the garage was hauled bodily from its temporary site on the main road to Pointe Baptiste. This was made the occasion of a public holiday. No wages were paid but cigarettes, and rum to the amount of about three gallons, were freely distributed. At seven in the morning, shells were blown to summon the people, but it was eleven before the great lumbering thing – it was rather a small garage, but any building, suddenly taking to itself legs would invite the epithets great and lumbering – began its lurching, staggering progress up the hill. Six palm trees were placed lengthwise in pairs on the road, and a wire rope, bound about with bark to prevent "misery of the hands", was attached to the front of the garage. A small boy was first on the line, than came the women, and then the men, a few strong men pushing behind.

Altogether there were about a hundred people on the job,

Hauling the garage – "a lurching staggering progress"

each haul lasting the length of a pair of tree trunks. A huge carpenter called Sam acted as officer-in-charge of the singers, and each song was most carefully timed to last the distance of a haul. Then came an interval for refreshment, while the trunks left behind were brought back to the front again. Giraud and Freddie were in charge of the rum, and at midday we inquired how the demijohn was holding out. Giraud whispered confidentially: "I water it a little, Sir. It is better so."

House moving was one of the few things that Dominicans did communally. The first time Holly Knapp saw house moving, to the sound of singing, he shouted: "Come, Percy, come Paul. We shall hear folk songs, traditional music; the real background of the people." But when he came close and could interpret what they were singing, he found it was: "Kaiser Bill's a bum."

As it was Lennox's business to supervise house building and produce vegetables so it was mine to be governess to our children, to make and mend their clothes. (Oh, the exasperation of the paper pattern, flipped into the garden by an impertinent wind; alternately, if there were no draught, adhering to a perspiring elbow.) Mine also the task of carrying on the family correspondence; and to amass, under impact of novelty, "material", which was afterwards used in articles for the Manchester Guardian and incorporated into my two novels. An Australian friend wrote: "We think you must mean you are keeping a dairy. Surely a diary wouldn't take much time?"

Pat and Michael found readjustment from nanny-in-the-nursery, Kensington-Gardens-in-the-pram, more difficult than I had anticipated. To me, beach and river were a constant adventure, desert-island fiction come true. My young had not been so assiduously conditioned to that type of literature. One afternoon they removed all their dolls and animals and camped on the red expanse of clay above Black Beach; and it seemed to me, as I surveyed them through field glasses, that nothing could so well have emphasised our change in surroundings as the sight of those Italian dolls with smug faces and curly mops, sitting on rocks left hitherto to sea birds.

Lessons were in one sense a fulltime job, on the principle of very little powder being administered in a great deal of jam, spread thinly over the day. Spelling games as we walked home from the river, jigsaw puzzles in the form of maps, French words given for the treasures of the beach. We laboured with Plasticine and coloured chalks, and on one unfortunate day I found in a magazine instructions for making a papier-mâché bowl by mixing shredded newspaper into a flour paste. This nauseating concoction Little Dog swallowed whole and was then sick.

Pat had already attended school in London, and we discovered that Michael could also read when, just after his fifth birthday, he pronounced "British Made" off a packing case. (There was a later phase when the Army and Navy Stores' catalogue was their favourite literature; and I overheard them choosing dresses for Pat in puce and marl and eau-de-nil.) Michael soon outstripped both of us in arithmetic. When utterly stumped I would have to call in

Pointe Baptiste with its 70ft veranda.

Lennox who, with the best of intentions, would make everything worse with his: "But it's so easy. You have only to put a figure here and an X so." Pat said: "I am not the sort of child who will ever need arithmetic, so why bother to teach me?"

Morning, noon, and night I read aloud to them as opportunity offered. Outgrown books were stored in a trunk which later was discovered to have become one enormous wood ants' nest so that many of our favourites had to be burned, together with a loathly mass of egg-laden, squirming, ochre-bellied insects which crawled in a brown flaky pastry made of digested paper and cardboard. It was hard not to be physically sick as the creatures emerged from their tunnels and spread over wooden and cement floorings, running frantically to escape.

Dominican wood ants are akin to the white ants I knew in

Australia and Africa, but ours are of an inferior type, mere poor relations, whose chocolate-coloured nests, hanging on tree or rafters, are more vulnerable than those remembered from other places. We offered the children threepence for any nest found in the vicinity, and portions of these would be thrown to the fowls who gobbled greedily at the fleeing insects. It was no hardship to be woken at half-past five to tell stories; to be compelled to see the sun rise, when the valleys and precipices of Morne aux Diables were exposed in a crumpled pattern never visible except at dawn. Every morning we bathed before breakfast at Grand Baptiste, where the seagrapes, which had been razed by Clifford together with his manchineel tree, had sprouted again and in the autumn bore a purple and unpalatable fruit.

There was no dependable rise and fall of tide. Sometimes for weeks on end there would be no variation and then, without obvious reason such as a new or full moon, one might walk precariously among sea eggs which thrust vicious black spikes six or eight inches into the air. On a coral so delicate that it crumbled underfoot there were shallow pools wherein lay sea slugs whose insides were like vermicelli, poisonous sea centipedes and octopi whose spite and defiance and courage when teased with a stick were out of all proportion to their size. Once we saw a very small one walking along the sand looking for all the world like a very bent old man on crutches. The local peasants called the octopus a sea-cat and was regarded by some as a great delicacy. I have never seen nor heard of large ones, large enough to be dangerous, but I remember a medium-sized one, squirming all over the floor, having been brought into the kitchen by a gourmet; with the servants standing on stools and clutching their skirts like Victorian maidens frightened of a mouse.

In fact, as regards physical dangers, we were singularly fortunate. There are no crocodiles, no poisonous serpents and no constrictors big enough to molest anything but a chicken. The snake called *tête-chien*, sometimes eight feet long and feared unreasonably by women working in the fields, would bite only if trodden.

There were always red crabs in the beach house, ready to eat a bathing suit or a shoe left carelessly on the floor; and, in the sand, little transparent ones, scrabbled for by dogs. Hermit crabs are called "soldier", some so small as to be almost invisible, and others larger than my fist, with one protruding red or yellow claw. When disturbed these emit a definite bark, presumably caused by some internal scraping of body against shell. Once we were lucky enough to come upon the psychological moment of shell changing, when hermits of all sizes played general post, moving to new quarters as in the autumnal flitting between New York apartment houses. Hundreds of little scurrying crabs were for a few moments all naked and defenceless together. I think that someone must at the end – as in musical chairs – have been left over, like the one who took for his dwelling the discarded top of a cocktail shaker.

◼

If the beach was a constant adventure so was housekeeping. In those faraway days to which, in the hungry forties, we looked back to as a food paradise, we had local meat twice

*The celebration of the feast of St Peter on the beach
at Calibishie.*

a week and fish nearly every day. When, towards evening,
the little boats sailed home, and conch shells were blown,
then we knew that kingfish or flying fish or *ton* or the long
pale dorado would be available to all comers, or at least to
first comers, at three pence per pound. Sometimes a stray
fisherman, coming by the cliff path, which is no more than
a series of holes cut in the side of a precipice, would offer us
his catch.

For a while we had our own fishpot, a basket-like
contrivance baited with cassava roots and soursops or with
an emerald-green moss. Stones served as weights, and were
secured to each corner with a rope made of vines. Generally
when there was a glut from other sources this would yield an
assortment of queer-shaped, queer-coloured, queer-tasting
fish with names meaning nothing to us. But we made the
mistake of employing, to empty our fishpots, the man who

made them at a dollar apiece and after every night of rough weather it would be reported that the pot was lost or "mashed up". So our fish became altogether too expensive. Owing to bad weather, the trap once lay for two days on the beach, and when Lennox went down with Bennett to re-set it, they found a wild cat imprisoned. There was no way of extracting the creature. It would not be coaxed, nor was it possible to lay hands on it. The men could only hold the trap under water until the savage beast was drowned.

Bread was baked twice a week in the cement oven standing beside a little village house trimmed with blue shutters. Roses and gardenias and huge pink lilies blew their scent across the road. Etiennette, blue frocked and bare legged, carried the loaves in a yellow basket. The loaves were more like rolls than what we call bread, tough and unleavened, a penny for small ones, threepence for large. Butter came out of a tin, but we bought milk from Ambrosine's stepfather – relationships are hard to keep track of in this land of few marriages and many "outside" children – which was delivered slightly watered in a vermouth bottle, having been drawn from the cow by a man's two fingers (to use both hands for milking was so unusual as to be matter for comment).

Twice a week, on an average, the milk bottle might fail to materialise. Either the cow was lost, or the calf had found her, or the messenger was "dancing last night and so he could not come". The priest told us that he once grumbled to a child: "I know half of this milk came out of the sea." And the child answered indignantly: "My father fill it he-self from the river." And there is that other tale of a bottle delivered only half full, and the bearer justifying himself with: "How could I fill it, Sir? The river is brown with flood water." When I scolded Looby, who should have known better, for bringing me watered milk, he said he had not put water into the bottle, but because the cow was tethered close to the river she had doubtless been drinking it.

It surprised us to find that fruit was cheaper out of season than in, as though a freak were something to be ashamed of. A rare January pineapple, for instance, might cost threepence, but in June sixpence. In winter a hunter might bring us a *ramier*, a wood pigeon; or a *perdrix*, which is not a partridge but a species of dove. And once only, although we see them often, rising to the surface between waves, a young turtle was given to us, swimming round and round in a barrel. In the interests of humanity, we quickly killed it and made it into soup, soup not quite as aldermen eat it but, with enough sherry added, edible. Turtle eggs – sticky and gelatinous, looking like ping-pong balls – were frequently laid on White Beach where there was a green seaweed pleasing to turtle mothers. In our first summer, Freddie found 140 eggs all buried together, and showed us a scar on a tree where the female had rubbed against it while laying. On the sand there were marks of feet and a shallow depression scoured out by the creature's body.

Breeding rabbits as a source of food has never been very successful. A bright lad in our village suggested: "They should be left free. It seems that method has been found satisfactory in Australia." When our first doe was brought to us, "not as a present but to sell," Ambrosine said, "she go to make children," which as it turned out was not true. That afternoon I took a drinking pan to her hutch among the fowls and the men mocked me, saying: "She no use water." To which I replied: "You mean she prefers rum?"

It is a fact that Dominicans did not believe that their beasts, be they cats or sheep or pigs, require more water than the raindrops cupped in leaves. Peasants are conspicuously not stock minded. A cow, for instance, will be tied to a stake on some one else's land and a shilling a month paid in grazing rent. If the weather is fair the position of the stake may be moved daily, which process is called "changing my cow". But if storm or flood or a more amusing engagement prevent, then the cattle may well be left standing for many days in a bare circle of trampled mud.

Tiny flies ravaged our ankles and the children scratched their bites, which went septic, as did cuts from razor grass. Where cattle had grazed one was liable to *bête rouge*, a larval mite whose attacks gave the effect of fleabites. There was a continual bathing of sores, an interminable bandaging and washing of bandages, the trying of different ointments which Holly called salves. It was as though the turned earth and the lopped trees had released a malevolence. In moments of despair I imagined that the land we loved so much did not like us. When we consulted the Irish doctor in Marigot, his sole contribution to the problem was: "It happens in Dominica." And so the expression – it happens in Dominica – became with a shrug of the shoulders part of our language, explaining, almost justifying, everything.

Sores and fevers, boils and blights, apathy and intrigue, madness and disaster happen in Dominica and there is nothing on God's earth that you can do about it. Ambrosine suggested putting aloes on our sores and produced a long cactus leaf from which she cut fleshy slices like pieces of jellyfish. When the bandages were removed in the morning the aloe had dried to the consistency of very thin paper and the pus had been absorbed.

It was as well that we had brought with us a considerable pharmacopoeia because carpenters and labourers were constantly asking for drugs – quinine, iodine, worm powders. "Since three days I have a grub which troubles my stomach. Please, Sir, to give me a dose to cure him." Bennett told me one day that the bowels of his friend were troubling him and requested Epsom Salts. We happened to be out of this valuable commodity, but "It is no matter," Bennett said. "He ask me already on Monday, and I forget. He can wait until Friday."

Some believed in leeches as a cure for influenza or headache, and I have seen small boys collecting them from among leaves in a swamp. Others trusted in powdered cockroaches, and said that rain falling on Good Friday must be gathered and applied to wounds. Shakespearean remedies were not altogether out of date – "Eye of newt and toe of frog, wool of bat and tongue of dog." Many Caribs vouched for the good effects of one's own or another's urine, drunk warm, as a cure for poisoning or stomach ache while others chewed the gum of the gommier tree to improve their wind. An aphrodisiac known as *poudre pine tortue* (powdered turtles' penis) was made and sold.

It was five months before any of us caught cold, here called "draught". On the orders of Anthony the carpenter, we all gargled with hot water and vinegar in which a tomato floated, and because we spat over the veranda rail there eventually sprouted tomato plants in the drain.

In the beginning, probably because he was over-anxious and harried, Lennox suffered from boils. Ambrosine suggested a mixture of soursop leaves and candle grease, but this was not as effective as her aloe treatment, and for a time "the master" could walk only with the greatest difficulty. Then Anthony took charge of the situation, ordering a poultice made of *farin*, cassava flour, and the fleshy inside of prickly pear leaves. These ingredients he supplied himself, and there was no doubt that the pain and swelling were considerably relieved.

Mr Dondie, a furniture-maker, came to call, expressing sympathy with Lennox's condition and saying that he also suffered from pimples. Considering that Lennox's leg was swollen like a full moon sprouting volcanoes, we felt the word pimple to be inadequate, bearing the same relation as a molehill to a mountain. Mr Dondie was a local character, who made the children a table and small chairs, and bored nine holes in the wooden seats of the latter. When I asked him why he had done this he told me: "For flourish." This also became part of our language, a phrase applied to any ornamentation or superfluity.

"Dominica meets you either with boils or fever," warned the old English major who lived near Marigot, and who often came down in the bus of a Saturday morning – beard flowing in the breeze, khaki trousers worn over a pseudo Jaeger singlet – carrying a bottle of milk and two bananas in a knapsack in case nobody invited him to lunch. The major prided himself on his likeness to Bernard Shaw but not to the extent of vegetarianism. It was piteous, and at the same time startling, to see what a prodigious amount of food he could put away, storing up like a camel against the week or fortnight he would have to eat at his own expense.

"Boils or fever," he said, meaning malaria, which troubled us all in our time. For the first four years I myself was immune, and then attacked no more than every six months, which I looked upon as slimming. But when, perhaps under the stress of grievous worry, the thing hit me every six weeks I was less amused: in my aunt's house near Paris, shivering and sweating under red satin hangings and recovering on a diet of white wine and peaches; in a Bloomsbury boarding house, listening all night to the grumbling of aeroplanes, or, in Switzerland, to the distant whistling of trains in a sanatorium where the room was white from the outside snow and the girls in the laboratory thanked me for giving them a new bug to look at. Then, I have seen in my mind's eye a little sluggish stream reaching the sand through red scum, mosquitoes breeding in crab holes under palm trees, and a copper *taish*, a bowl formerly used for boiling sugar, full of rain water where the Anopheles wrigglers swim upright like microscopic sea horses.

5 A new design for living

If the tale of house building be out of proportion to the whole, allowance must be made for the impact of novelty. We were learning a new design for living, the ways of a new people.

When we left London, one friend said: "How terrible to think of Lennox and Elma spending the rest of their lives drinking rum on a veranda." And another said, "I could do with a little lotus-eating myself." But of course it wasn't like that at all. No lotuses were within reach, and we still drank whisky. Not until the war years did we switch over to rum. Seldom, in fact, had we been so busy. But what we did, we did together, free of the tyranny of the office, of the rushed departure of the breadwinner after breakfast, of his weary return too late for the children's visit to the drawing room.

On the evening our furniture arrived, almost the first thing to emerge from among crockery and books and lampshades, all stacked higgledy-piggledy in the new kitchen, was the full-length mirror. Secretly, I took stock of myself. My hair was long and ragged, my face shiny. I was considerably thinner than I remembered. Now that I am more plump than I could wish, and English friends are scornful from within their girdles, the village people say admiringly: "Madame is so beautifully stout." I had developed neither boils nor fever. I seemed to be healthier than ever before. (I was astonished, when, years later, looking through old letters that came to me on the death of my mother-in-law, to see how often I complained of feeling tired.) But I had been more tired in London, tired by buses and tube trains, by hairdressers and the pursuit of clothes. Here I was never so tired that I could not delight in my surroundings, be pleased by an unusual sunrise, by the outline of the French islands, by mist swirling out of the valleys of Morne Diablotin. My feet had coal-black sand to tread on, red cliffs, and a coral reef. They had to my mind more value than all the grey pavements of cities.

Lennox and I had not come to the West Indies to be sociable. I had brought no grand dresses. It was said of me with bated breath: "She dined on board the Lady Boat in a cotton frock." For the sake of the children, however, and because we were welcomed with great kindness and considerable astonishment – everybody thought us mad to build this house "behind God's back" – we had to mix with our white neighbours, who were alien enough in all conscience, and few in number.

There was one hearty planter, more typically the retired sergeant-major than one could believe, and another, lean as though he wrestled with the devil, carrying a huge Adam's

apple and a sense of sin. The assistant agricultural officer
had been torn by some bureaucratic quirk from his real job
as a schoolmaster. The doctor was a mad Irish theosophist,
who lent me books about ghosts and fairies, but never saw
any. "How wonderful it would be," I said, "to have second
sight here." And he looked at me in a vague bewildered sort
of way saying: "Do you suppose anything interesting ever
happened in Dominica?" Which is saturated with history
and old, unhappy far-off things: battles between French and
English, massacres of Caribs, burying of treasure, and
slaying of the diggers lest they reveal the hiding place.

Among these people were two little girls and two little
boys with whom Pat and Michael had perforce to be friends.
The children were dominated by a formidable, childless
character, who dropped her aitches and once called on us at
ten in the morning complete with gloves and calling cards.
She kept the ladies of the north, white or coloured, under a
dictator's thumb, so that they dared not make so much as a
cake except to her recipe. There was the young and shy
parson trying to buy what she had called an 'air mattress,
and he in all good faith asking her: "Show me where you
blow it up." And the notorious telephone embroilment of:
"I'm sending you an 'en." Louder and louder, "An 'en, man
an 'en," with a quiet background accompaniment from her
husband of: "Try calling it a fowl, dearie."

Elsewhere in the island there were other odd characters.
Andrew Green, for instance, an American engineer who
built himself a palace near Roseau and is still remembered
for his pertinent phrases. "Dominica is the island where the
impossible always happens, and the inevitable never takes

place", while he described the white shrine overlooking the town as: "Like the Bishop's mind, all spike, and very little Jesus." Andrew was buried at his own insistence in one of his own lime fields. But his widow afterwards had the place consecrated and made cemetery-like, with an ornamental wall and symmetrical shrubs, which was everything that Andrew would not have wanted. When, a year or so later, it was proposed to make an airfield on that piece of unusually flat land it was found that holy ground would be in the middle of it.

Judge Pemberton was another figure from those early days who we visited at Pointe Mulâtre on the east coast. Peacocks, white and blue, roosted in mango trees, and deer of his own importing strayed invisibly on the forested hillsides, descending to feed off gardens, and being shot by peasant farmers.

Arriving at three o'clock, hot and tired and longing for a nice cup of tea, I was sat down before three bottles of rum, and told to sample all of them, and pronounce which was the best. Knowing nothing whatever about rum I voted for the one most resembling brandy, and by the grace of God chose right.

The judge was an alarming person with an alarming reputation, and was at that time chary of tourists, having been recently written about by Alec Waugh to his great displeasure. A West Indian of good family, Pemberton had retired to his plantation partly to nurse grievances and partly to allow legends to ripen about him. But it was no legend that the mangosteen trees which he had spent 40 years in bringing to perfection had been destroyed by a hurricane in

40 minutes, and for 16 years before he died, the judge never left Pointe Mulâtre.

Social intercourse in the Northern district, before the invention of the cocktail party at which one never drinks cocktails, was by elaborate picnic. The few white families were not on friendly terms with each other, and the miasma of ill feeling was doubtless more easily dissipated in the open air. Two white couples, and two only, were living in the neighbourhood of Portsmouth and these were rigidly not on speaking terms. This was a case of female jealousy in the matter of precedence, one lady being the wife of a plantation manager and the other of the magistrate and district officer. When a local bridge was formally opened, these representatives of big business and the state ran forward as though in a race, scissors open, each hoping to assert their rank by cutting the tape first.

Masqueraders at Pointe Baptiste during carnival time.

Twenty miles away, two other white couples spoke to each other rarely and only at long intervals, while the substance of their quarrel was lost in the mists of time. A jetty came into it, a right of usage rather than a right of way. An ex-governor of the Leeward Islands had already written in his memoirs: "Dominica is a strange island of likes and dislikes, and perhaps to some extent nerves. For the brooding overhanging mountains, exhilarating enough when one is living on the heights, exert at times a curiously depressing effect on those living in the closed in valleys." When I suggested to one of our neighbours that she should call me by my first name, she answered: "We are against being on Christian name terms in Dominica. It makes it so awkward when we quarrel."

Woodford Hill beach, where a great sweep of white sand was protected from the road by a tangle of seagrape and almonds, was the favourite place for picnics. The sluggish river, after flowing among *mang* trees hung with lianas, met the sea under a cliff on top of which was windblown turf, and bushes forced by the north-east trades into uniform shapes as though shorn by clippers. Here was a rocky broken coast where foam lingered in little pools or rushed back into the ocean by a thousand crevices bored in grey rocks; while under the cliff there was masonry embedded in the coral and a rusty capstan to show where had once been a jetty. Fishermen beached their boats by an old wall, and as they sailed past or dismantled their craft, one realised how beautiful against a blue sea are black, strong-muscled bodies compared to pinky-white ones sitting on sand.

When a visitor from overseas, or even from the other side

of the island, gave "society" an excuse, it assembled at Woodford Hill to consume prodigious quantities of food: sausage rolls and sandwiches, patties and pastries, sugared buns and raisin tarts. Cakes and jams set the standard of social achievement, and were a prime source of rivalry. It was traditional among the white ladies not to allow their servants to bake as though, in these days of education for everyone, they would have lost their last supremacy, their racial superiority.

At picnics, as at most parties, there was rigid segregation of the sexes except during the actual process of eating. Once the administrator's wife caught me chatting with two Methodist parsons and called me away saying: "You're losing your reputation." Women talked servants and cake while men discussed politics and planting. (Once, I asked why, in the West Indies, persons practising agriculture were always called "planters" and was told: "because they plant and never reap.") If talk in a small colony seems to be limited and local, one reason may be that however frequently persons may meet, seeing not only the social side of each other but, like fish in an aquarium, all round and too often, they have not remotely the same background. They are brought together not by natural selection but by sheer accident and have to make the best of it.

Our friend Holly, well-read, well-educated, and full of wit and malice, who had been football coach in one of the smart American private schools, who had emigrated to Tahiti, drifted to Tonga and then to Dominica, was determined to lead his own peculiar life in his own way, and would not mix with the Northern district gentry but only with the village. I could see his point, but then he had no children whom he thought it his duty to keep in contact with the wider world.

The worst thing that ever happened at a Woodford Hill picnic was that the children climbed a manchineel tree. Pat did not venture far and was only slightly burned on hands and mouth. But by next morning Michael and some other boys had high temperatures and fat grey blisters as large as pigeons' eggs and full of loathsome yellow matter, behind knees and thighs, and when these broke they left raw wounds. There were very few manchineel trees remaining in Dominica, and no one had known this one was there. The early settlers had cut them down for fear of poisoned arrows and the obeah masters.

I do not believe that obeah was ever so powerful a force in Dominica as in Jamaica or Haiti. There were, however, hints, undercurrents, suggestions, as when Clifford and Cozier decided a spell had been put upon our vegetable garden. It is as foolish to deny the existence of something merely because you have not seen it as to say "It can't happen here" because it suddenly may. Cozier, although a staunch Protestant, was a hotbed of notions and superstitions. He told us that he would never dare to steal because the people would always find him out by magic; and when his own sheep was stolen he gave the priest a candle to burn which would cause the thief to go on stealing recklessly until he was caught.

"But", said Lennox, setting aside for the moment the immorality of such a device, "you are a Methodist. How can a priest burn candles for you?" Shamefaced, Cozier admitted that he had persuaded a Catholic friend to arrange it.

When Holly was robbed – his cash box being bodily removed, while he was in his kitchen – Clifford suggested that he should find a clever man to draw a picture and then shoot at it. "Within a month, boss, the thief will surely die." Our first reaction was that it might be amusing to try. Then we realised that if some poor innocent should chance to die from natural causes, he would go to his grave under shadow of a crime. Quite early in our West Indian life we learned that one may ward off the effects of obeah by putting garlic between the toes.

The French priest in the nearby village of Wesley, the same one who had lost his temper with Brussels sprouts that would not sprout and had slashed their heads off with a cutlass while shouting the Breton equivalent of "That'll larn yer", only to discover they immediately "larned" and sprouted, told us that he had found a bottle with two little dolls in it hanging on the last grave in the cemetery. A white doctor had recently married a coloured girl and this device had been chosen as a means of punishing the miscegenation, as it must cause the principal characters to die. (And indeed they did die, as do most of us, she from TB and he later, in London, during an air raid.)

"The next day after mass," said the priest, "I open the bottle in church and empty it of their rubbish before them all. I show them, pfui, what I think of their obeah."

In the beginning we heard more of such things than we do now. Superstitious practices are out of place in this new world of certified midwives and police stations, of school examinations and DDT. Or were we in those early days more receptive, more credulous, as though in curiosity we stirred the stagnant pools of the forest which are spread with a rainbow scum and hide something called "yosophie", which causes itching of the feet? Since the war, the village has talked in terms of shifting cultivation and praedial larceny; of slave mentality and the universal franchise; and debating whether it was the imperial principle of world economics that kept us in poverty.

I realise, looking back, that we had made our entrance in Dominica at the end of an act, when the orchestra was already playing the overture to a new one. To us it was faintly absurd, altogether out of the escapist's pictures, to find modes and manners controlled by Eminent Victorians. Gloves and stockings, silver salt cellars and tea equipages, the White Man's Burden and the prestige of the Master Race, all these were part of a tradition stretching back to the French wars and beyond when, in the minds of Englishwomen, there was fear of "going to pieces in the tropics".

This attitude was rigidly maintained until the tide of democracy and commonsense, to say nothing of war conditions, swept it away. Just before the war, an English girl, who had married a man of colour and who came to reside in Roseau, announced that her in-laws should be quite especially considerate of her because "a white woman disintegrates so quickly in the tropics". I remember her husband's uncle wuffling like a cross pug dog: "I won't have that woman disintegrating in my house." Mixed marriages have become more frequent; and in my day if we had not danced and dined and laughed with coloured people we should have had a very dull time.

When our house was finished, we were free to explore, to pursue rivers and ridges to their ultimate conclusions, although in fact we seldom came to the source of a stream or to the ending of a track. Once we asked an old man: "How far can we go by this path?" And we were told, "You can go as far as you can get."

I myself have never "got". But once upon a time, Michael, by then a young man, tried to climb Morne Diablotin from that ridge where we had met the old man, and was absent for four days, finding the path peter out into a "flat" of untouched forest. At something over 3,000 feet he was checked by caclin through which it would have taken many men many days to hack a passage. Caclin (*clusia venosa*) is at low altitudes a parasite plant with glossy leaves and a plum-like fruit edible to birds only; but it also forms part of what botanists call "the elfin or mossy woodland of the high peaks".

Anthony Trollope visiting the West Indies in the guise of a postmaster, wrote in his diary: "Dominica, from the sea, fills one with an ardent desire to be off and rambling among those green mountains; as if one could ramble through such wild country; or ramble at all with the thermometer at eighty five." This mere dot on the map, whose area is estimated at 300 square miles, is in fact so enormous, its crumpled hills and valleys so many and so diverse that no one could see all of them in a lifetime unless he gave mind and body to nothing else. It is an everlasting delight to ramble, and the thermometer is not always at 85°F.

There were very few motorable roads when we came to Dominica. To know the island one had to walk, making three or four-day excursions. We ourselves found plenty to explore in our own north-east corner, classifying the little single-file tracks into ridge paths, garden paths and fishermen's paths. The latter were situated on the edge of precipices, and often led to a "look-out" 200 feet above sea level, or sometimes to an estuary where half a dozen boats, a couple of rafts, lay side by side on shingle. Ridge paths, obviously, kept to the highest places and were old hunters' trails beaten by wild pigs, whereon we have found deep pits serving as traps. The French made paved tracks for their ox carts, and these were graded to curve round and about hills, which the Caribs had taken the hard way. Some of these roads have been rebuilt and some are lost and forgotten so that one may come unexpectedly in the forest upon stretches of *pavé* without end or beginning. Garden paths followed the beds of rivers, crossing and re-crossing the streams as most convenient to the lie of the land, and linking provision grounds in the middle of which might stand a breadfruit or an old gommier, the latter preserved for its sap which lights a fire or makes a flambeau.

Constantly we were appalled by the wanton destruction of the forest, by the pillage and rapine caused by "shifting cultivation", the squatting on Crown Lands. During the first world war these had been thrown open to the indiscriminate use of the peasants. It was a policy, perhaps necessary at the time, but it had cost the island dear in the loss of timber, in

Elma and Patricia on White Sand Beach. Home schooling included "French words given for the treasures of the beach."

the spoilation of fertile acres. All through the dry season, known as the carême, we would see smoke rising from hill and valley as the flames swept over the newly cleared gardens. Then the pattern of the mountainside would be altogether changed. In the abandoned plantations there would spring up wild eggplant and castor oil and razor grass. Eventually, tree ferns or shoots of *bois rivière*, sprouting from an old stump, would bring back a semblance of woodland but never the old warriors of the virgin forest. Seeds and seedlings had perished by fire. Protest or suggestion were to no avail. "That may be so in England, Madame, but not in Dominica."

In the Hodges valley, hidden under a dull green creeper called volcan, the seeds of which are supposed to have floated to Dominica in 1902 with ashes from the volcanic eruption of Mont Pelée in neighbouring Martinique, we found, a rampart of stones built up by Canadian lumbermen in the 1880s. "An expensive dam was made," so says Sir Robert Hamilton in his 1894 report on conditions in

Dominica, "in order to bring down logs. It cost several hundred pounds and was utterly useless." Freddie remembered the making of this as a schoolboy. "The river mash it up," he told us, "and they build it back and again the river mash it. And at last they go away." So it has been, not once nor twice, in our fair island story.

On the knife-edged ridges, tracks are likely to be interrupted by masses of rock, huge, out of all proportion to their surroundings, as though they might be fortresses made by man; and these are split by roots into crevices from which sprout ferns and parasite leaves, like those of an aspidistra, called *z'ailes mouches*, which were used long ago to thatch Carib houses. And there are orchids of no particular beauty or importance. For it is wrong to suppose that orchids are always in flaming colours, being sometimes little scrubby things like withered ling, a corolla of pale beige, or a mist of lilac on the twigs of a dead lime tree. Those gigantic rocks are also found in rivers, into which they may have rolled during earthquakes. But whether those left on the high ridges were spat from a volcano in some tremendous cataclysm, or whether softer stones have been eroded all round, leaving them most fit survivors of more exalted places, I am too ignorant to know.

◪

The first time we ever went into the Carib Reserve, walking the red clay track from the Pagua river it was to return a visit which the chief, who called himself king, had made us while we were still living in Paul's *moulin* with Knapp. Percy Agar came with us, and Eleanor Early, an American travel writer, who hoped to take photographs for a possible magazine article. I remember a picturesque old dame in grey rags, carving calabashes, who was coy at the idea of being snap-shotted protesting that she was "*trop sale, trop laide*". But when fully convinced that we really wanted the picture she said: "You pay me?" And when offered sixpence demanded a shilling, which was more than a day's wage, had there been work and wages available. By the time Percy had paid for three photographs he was asking Eleanor, "What do you expect to make out of this article anyway?

The Caribs are a small and sturdy people with straight black hair and copper-coloured complexions paling to a shade of putty or darkening to bronze. Only the faces of the men, the blue-black tresses of the women, and their slanting eyes, remind one that these are the remnant of a once powerful race, the descendants of a people who so successfully defied Spaniards, French and English that – in the scramble for the Antilles – Dominica was declared neutral because no one could conquer it.

Only in Dominica do any true Caribs survive at all. Impenetrable valleys and inhospitable coasts prevented the extermination inevitable in more accessible islands; and the Carib strain must be very strong for all over the island, but of course especially on the windward coast, one still recognises their Mongolian type features, hearing "So-and-So is a red man", and "That red girl living on the ridge." There is no wall around the reserve, no frontier post nor even boundary mark. The track widens, the bay trees beside it stand thick and close as though they were a stockade or a defence. There is a sense of withdrawal, of reticence.

Fifteen minutes off the main road, there is a settlement called Bataca, of wooden houses, sugar-thatched or with shingled roofs, huddling under breadfruit and mango trees. It is a village seldom visited, essentially reserved, where the people were farouche among their pigs and fowls and naked children. They were reputed to be unfriendly, even to other Caribs among whom they were known for treachery and for the practice of magic.

The better-known village of Salybia lies two or three valleys away in an amphitheatre of green mountains, red-scarred where the road is, or where the earth has slid from under the protecting mantle of the forest. A few grey buildings, a church, a school, a presbytery, had been set up on what, from the hill above, appeared to be a smooth lawn

Carib chief, Jolly John, and family photographed during a visit by the Napiers to the Carib Reserve, home of Dominica's indigenous people.

crossed by a strip of dark foliage masking a river where crabs came out to play with children in a shadowy gorge. In the lee of high cliffs, boats were drawn up on a harsh beach of pebbles at which the surf pounded and crashed. Once a month, a French priest sailed the rough sea, or rode over the hills, to say mass at the altar of St Mary of the Caribs.

There was no longer, even 30 years ago, any authentic folklore. No song or dance or costume distinguished the Caribs from any other inhabitant of Dominica. Only their waterproof baskets were still called "Indian", woven in lovely patterns of brown and black and cream; and high in the forest, men made dugout canoes which were hollowed from a gommier tree felled at the new moon. This would be felled with an axe, hauled to the sea by many men singing, and there filled with stone and water for the process of widening.

Chief Thomas Jolly John was Japanese in appearance, small and as mild-mannered a master of a tribe as could be imagined. On his original visit to Pointe Baptiste, he had sat motionless and silent for nearly an hour, drinking rum whenever so invited. When, at last, our uninvited guest revealed the purpose of his call, he asked us to protest to the Aborigine Society against the rude things said of him in the official report on the Carib incident of 1930 about which, at that time, we knew absolutely nothing. It appeared that the police, justifiably suspecting the Caribs of smuggling, had made a raid on the reserve. The Caribs had defended their goods and defied arrest; the police, beaten and bruised, were driven out and Jolly John, Pilate-like, had washed his hands of the whole affair. The Caribs sustained casualties of two killed and two injured, the result of revolver shots fired by the police.

I believe that the subsequent excitement was terrific. Throughout the island, people talked wildly of a Carib rising. A British warship, which had been lurking below the horizon during the celebration of carnival, was sent round to make a display of force. Star-shells were fired and there was a display of searchlights, whereupon the Caribs, unaccustomed to these evidences of civilisation, rushed from their houses and took refuge in the woods. An inquiry was demanded, a commission sat, and the report smacked everybody's head a little and the Carib chief's hardest of all. He was degraded from his position, while his staff of office or "mace" was removed to Roseau. He was forbidden to call himself king.

Now we found him building himself a new house on the slope above Salybia. The earth around about it had been scratched into a semblance of a flower garden where croton bushes had been thrust to root in the bare ground, and cosmos and zinnia seedlings struggled under the sun. Inside the one room – there was an alcove curtained off for sleeping – were a few hard and strangely ecclesiastical-looking chairs and a table whereupon lay three books: the Bible in English, a Petit Larousse Illustre, and an agricultural handbook. Over the door hung little charms, strips of stuff binding crossed sticks.

A few days afterwards Jolly John wrote to my husband: "I am constructing my new house for the entertainment of foreigners. Perhaps you would like to make a little contribution?" And again: "I am asking you to be good enough to lend me at least 10 dollar. I shall be very much obliged to you if you render me this service without jumping heart, as I will endeavour to refund it back in a very short time." (Years later another, younger, chief wrote to me asking for 50 dollars. "My little bananas is dirty", he pleaded, meaning unweeded, "and my mother is grown too old to work for me.")

In 1934, these people made one last protest against integration with the community. Contrary to their wishes and in defiance of local advice, the government put up a police station at Salybia. Before it was even finished, the Caribs made a Christmas bonfire of it piling tools and unused timbers on to the flames. "Lawlessness, pure lawlessness" was peasant opinion outside, "but indeed it was foolishness of guv'ment ever to set up a station, for the money saved by the stopping of smuggling would never pay the price of one policeman."

When things go wrong in Dominica, which they very frequently do, people talk of the Curse of the Caribs which does not necessarily mean the curse which the Caribs put on the white man, but reflects more probably the dying execrations of the mild-mannered Arawaks. Douglas Taylor, an English anthropologist who lived in Dominica for many years, and who knew more about these people than any of us, says that although there are no records it is probable that the first half of the 19th century was the period of the Caribs' final conversion to Christianity. This, too, was the time of the greatest decay in language, tradition, and custom. Certain English words in constant use such as hurricane, hammock, canoe, have been acquired from Carib.

Except for a few years of French conquest and occupation, Dominica has been under British rule since 1763, and yet we found that patois or Creole was still universally spoken. This is a language evolved in islands settled by the French by slaves who could not understand each other's languages. Similar Creole languages are spoken not only in Haiti and the French West Indies, but also in Mauritius and the Seychelles. Individual words are French, but construction and pronunciation is altogether different. For example, the R becoming W in our patois gives the impression of a lisp: "*Ou la bwé fwét mwe?* ("Where is my cold drink?") Verbs are not conjugated, always remaining the same no matter what tense is used: the present is expressed by ka. "*Mwen ka vini*"(I am coming) and the future by ke. "*Mwen ke vini demain.*" For the past one uses the verb alone, "*Mwen vini.*"

A French West Indian has written: "*Notre Creole*

Gardener Freddie Warrington with Robert, the donkey.

nationale merite une place dans l'art, dans l'universelle republique des lettres." But in Dominica our own educational authorities were of the opinion that "patois is of no cultural value, and there is no question of preserving a racial language as in Wales or Quebec." The first time I ever went into a village school I found a teacher from Nevis who could speak no patois endeavouring to instruct children who could speak no English. What could be more absurd? And yet, when I began to hear Calibishie children playing in the street in English I did, sentimentally and quite unreasonably, feel that something unusual and exotic was passing away.

In Dominica, it seems that English is the better for being a "learned" language, and is often curiously old-fashioned; it is the language, in fact, of Shakespeare and the Bible. But even among the educated, and even among expatriates, speech shows the French influence. The popular expletive *bon Dieu*, for instance; the *oui* at the end of a sentence which may be question or affirmative. "You go to town, *oui*?" answered by: "I go, *oui*," with a drop in tone. The convent schoolchildren will say: "Mother is *maudit* to set us so many sums." Often, there is a French twist to a sentence. The comparative, for instance, will be "more long" rather than longer, or "He work more fast" rather than faster. The inherent inertia of the people, that tired feeling, is reflected in the dropping of a word or syllable. The cow, for example, is "pounded" rather than impounded (found straying and put behind bars to be bailed out by a fine). "My garden is 'praised'," instead of appraised (valued by a village constable when someone else's animal has damaged it).

I am told that the curious use of the diminutive adjective

– "I go to buy my little provision" or "Madame, I beg you a little passage in your car" – comes from West Africa where the operative word is "small". But what the origin is of "so so" meaning "very well thank you", I cannot imagine. And if you are not in good health you say: "I not quite bright today."

6 Forest and river

Lennox and his cousin Ernest Simon, later Lord Simon of Wythenshawe, discovered the Chaudiere together. Following a "garden" path they came to a place where two rivers meet in virgin forest. The main stream tumbles 20 feet into a cut rock basin with high grey sides and, below this fall, to the width of a few feet, being compressed into a blue-green canyon of great depth wherein one may see mullet moving, and crayfish on the sandy bottom. There, the rocky banks are no longer clean-cut but seamed with moss, and fretted into hollows holding rain or flood water or sodden leaves; all within the green twilight of trees, for the sun reaches the Canyon pool for no more than an hour at noon, and even then the water is dappled with shadows. The smaller stream, called 'Ti Branche, is united to the larger by a cascade pouring into a deep hole so covered with a froth of bubbles that we named it the Champagne pool.

We picnicked once or twice in that place, and a few weeks

later found half its beauty destroyed. One side of 'Ti Branche had been cut flat to make a food garden: great trees axed and left lying one upon another like spillikins; and among the jagged stumps a few dasheen plants making green blots on a burned and blackened desolation. Elisha, a local man, had not wanted the trees for lumber, nor for fuel, nor to build a boat. What he could not clear off by burning he had left to rot.

We bought the Chaudiere not only because it was lovely, but to save the forest. At first we talked of 10 acres. Then Lennox applied for 20. One day, when I came back from a trip to Roseau he told me that the piece of land he wanted would be only 45 acres instead of 50. Nothing like 50 had ever been mentioned, but it is for that number that I now hold receipts. My husband had never, as a boy, had all the panache for which he craved and had reacted into extravagance. I often had to put on the brake, and now I regret bitterly that I ever worried meanly about little things.

Crown Land cost 10 shillings an acre, but with surveyors' fees it came to considerably more. We made the devastated area into a house site, and Elisha, who had cut the garden, gladly took a pound in compensation, with a few days' wages for clearing the mess he had himself created.

Space was borrowed to store timber at what was called Hampstead works, old grey buildings near the mouth of a river that has in the past been called both Bedford and Battibou. Carpenters prepared boards (I had thought we were quit of carpenters) and made beds and tables, and men carried these up river, walking the green aisles between coconut palms. It is about an hour's walk from the main road to the Chaudiere, crossing the river six times. The fords, named by numbers, have changed a little through the years. With each flood, stones are rolled into different places, a bank crumbles, dead trees dam one channel and set another free. Under the palm trees there are piles of dead coconuts collected for husking, the outer covering split by a sharp stake driven into the ground. Once upon a time we used to see the peeled nuts bobbing their way down the

Champagne pool (left) and Chaudron pool (below) at the Chaudiere, a piece of land bought by the Napiers "not only because it was lovely but to save the forest".

"canal" to be dried into copra at the works, where in the past limes were crushed by a great wheel, and cane was ground. Wherever there was a wheel there had to be an aqueduct carrying water to turn it. But they have turned very seldom in my time and the old stone waterways have been broken.

Beyond the sixth ford, cultivation came to an end and there was rough grass for pasture, with a few old mangoes and breadfruits planted long ago for slaves to eat. The latter tree was brought from Tahiti not, of course, in the Bounty but in HMS Providence. Whether the breadnut was imported at the same time I do not know, but it is a tree almost indistinguishable from the breadfruit, the leaf being slightly less serrated, the fruit more rugose. And inside, instead of doughy flesh, there are seeds reminiscent of chestnuts. It is a curious thing that although the tree is listed among those of Trinidad these delicious nuts are unknown in Jamaica and only rarely eaten in any of the other islands. A breadnut is never picked off the tree but is allowed to fall at the psychological moment. And if one be overlooked and left on the ground you may find a month or two later a cluster of miniature trees sprouting from a messy pulp.

Behind the two-roofed house that we built at the Chaudiere, Lennox planted grapefruit and oranges, which did very badly, and grafted mangoes and avocados that never fruited at all. The people said: "It is too cold," which in their phraseology means too wet. Mangosteens came into bearing after 14 years, and of the ornamental trees we put in for "flourish", a few grew into fine plants and flower in their season. But for most of them, the forest has been too

The house at the Chaudiere – "about an hour's walk from the main road...crossing the river six times".

powerful, casting out the exotic strangers. Only alamanda, and a pink congea, and a blue creeper called thunbergia have run wildly to the tops of trees, binding the branches together and, on the ground, slowly absorbing dead logs and razor grass and strangled hibiscus.

With children and grandchildren, or alone, I have spent time at the Chaudiere, finding precious the solitude of the forest, the liberty of the river. Few things in life have been more lovely than yielding to the current in the Canyon pool, floating face upwards in the soft water, looking to the sun, to the twisting lianas, to the green lace of tree fern. And just as at Pointe Baptiste there is always the sound of the sea – a roaring or a murmur or the sudden crash of a roller breaking prematurely – so at the Chaudiere there is always the even, monotonous sound of the river, rising in anger only after heavy rain.

Sometimes the sun shines all day on the dappled water. Then there is light and shade in the forest; pale green, dark green, emerald, olive; silver where the wind ruffles the leaves of the *bois flot*; brilliantly blue in a shower of petrea. But sometimes the rain is so strong that the trees are blotted from us and there is only water. Then we wait for the river to rise, for the gently pleasant stream to become a red and raging torrent, as though the forest bled of its wounds. At first there is faint discolouration, a spluttering over boulders that are normally dry. Lumps of foam spin slowly in a backwater. Then, if rain in the mountains be steady there will be a sudden grumbling noise, and, so swiftly that one never quite realises the precise moment of its happening, an avalanche of rust-red water will be pouring through the valley, and a little more of the good soil of Dominica will be carried out to sea.

Chaudiere is the peasants' name for the waterfall in 'Ti Branche, while the one in the main stream is called Chaudron, which my dictionary interprets as kettle, an innocuous word to represent so turbulent a flow of water, so much froth and bubble. Chaudiere, meaning boiler, is more expressive. Between these are the pools called Canyon and Centre, for places must be identified, and we thought it amusing to keep to the letter C.

There have been long lovely days, wading, stumbling, climbing after husband or son, carrying in one hand dead mullet by a forked stick through their gills, and in the other bait of avocado pear protected with difficulty from a greedy dog. It is said that in Dominica fish will take a fly, but I have never seen it done, the more usual bait being a green grasshopper, or a little brown cricket found in shut-up places. I have known Michael to go out in the dark with cutlass and *flambeau* and return at midnight with fish who had risen to their death from secret deeps and crevices lured by the light of flames. Unsporting? No, because so very difficult to kill on the wing. The peasants' way of fishing is by cast net or dynamite, and now in the modern fashion by gun. Twice I have seen the *titiree* or young fry swarm and crawl over the rocks beside the waterfalls, a black wriggling mass of migrating fish passing up river, each one no more than an inch long, the weakest and the most foolish falling by the wayside, left on dry stones most terribly to stink. *Titiree*, clear as crystal when they leave the sea, may be caught in estuaries by a sack being thrown over them; fried in breadcrumbs, they make a most passable imitation of whitebait.

There have been other days at the Chaudiere, no less lovely but more restful, spent on the veranda watching birds fish instead of men, *crabier* and *gaulin*, solemn and pernickety and heron-like; and those swift, grey kingfishers who nest in banks. The thrush called trembler shivers and shakes with a perpetual ague, carrying in its song the sound of an English summer; and this bird develops a certain impertinence for I have known one to tweak my toes as I sat sewing. Hummingbirds, with garnet or emerald throats, fly and appear motionless, hovering in front of a flower as though to mesmerise it before probing; while the chicken hawk called *malfini* swoops slowly, gracefully, over the

*Elma and Michael
outside the kitchen
at the Chaudiere –
"the solitude of the
forest, the liberty of
the river".*

treetops, making a cry like a creaking spar (it was chosen by
the Caribs as an emblem so that to become a chieftain a
young man must swallow the gall bladder after killing it).
At dawn or dark there may be a screeching of parrots. Bush
mosquitoes sting in the daytime but vanish punctually at
sunset. And I wonder, do they die at dusk, those who survive
my irritation? Or do they creep back into the wet places that
bred them, into a cow's footprint or into the red and yellow,
lobster-like claws of the *balisier*?

At night there is only the river, with sometimes the
metallic beat of the blacksmith beetle to join the chorus of
frog and cricket, which is now so much part of my life that
I never notice it.

On stay-at-home days, loyalty engenders hope that one's man will come home successfully from his fishing, but laziness would prefer that there would be no mullet to grill by torchlight, or to fry with head and tails protruding from a too small pan. Always, if the loved one be late, and the sun goes behind the western ridge, there comes a little niggling fear, for the woods and pools are lonely, and he might break a leg and no one know.

Woodford Hill picnics and my teaching notwithstanding, the children had to go away to school. Pat being two years older than Michael was the first. She had been pleased to go until the very night we set sail for Barbados, from which moment until I left her there six days later, she hardly spoke and never ate. Is it really necessary, I wonder, even though some enjoy boarding school, that tradition should inflict such recurrent torture upon us and upon our children?

After Pat's first Christmas holidays, she was ill in the sanatorium, and wrote so miserably that I rushed down to her bedside, making one of those little-bit-out-of-the-ordinary voyages that one remembers more vividly than conventional ones.

There was no mail boat for a week, but a Norwegian freighter was due the morning after I arrived in Roseau. The agent told me she would be in at dawn and sailing at half-past six. "If you want a passage," he said, "you must be there. Some of the captains won't take passengers at all. I never knew one to take a woman." At half-past four I crept out of Percy Agar's house near the village of Loubiere and walked down the hill. There was an old moon overhead, and the Southern Cross hung low. Far out at sea I could see a single light. In the village, there was a taxi waiting, parked among a litter of black pigs. On the main road a dog barked frantically at tiny waves made silver by the moonlight; or perhaps he was seeing some spirit returned to the scene of old battles.

I was on the Roseau jetty by half-past five. Almost imperceptibly the stars faded, one by one. Suddenly and simultaneously the lights of the town were extinguished. A little battered ship came slowly to her anchorage. Her hull was camouflaged because, someone said, that she had once been a rum-runner. Half an hour later the agent signalled with his thumbs up. "For 10 dollars," he said, "the cabin is yours."

There was a red saloon upholstered in velvet with snow scenes on the wall. The tablecloth was in grey and orange checks. Brass spittoons were anchored under the chairs. In the narrow cabin a torn green blind sheltered the porthole; and over the washbasin there was pinned last year's calendar featuring a blonde and lipsticked female whose cheeks were touched with a pale mildew. All morning I sat in sunshine on a deck that seemed to be mine alone, reading the autobiography of HG Wells which Holly had bought in Bermuda; he had been delighted to find that the English edition was half the price of the American one until he realised that the English version was in two volumes of which he now had only one for his money. The other passenger stood in the shadow cast by the bridge. A German from Montreal, bound for British Guiana, he had heard of my need to go to Barbados, and immediately resigned the cabin. Coatless, collarless, mopping a sun-blistered face and neck, he made a singularly un-prepossessing knight errant.

Slow, silent hours resolved the blue triangle that was Martinique into sudden peaks and dark valleys, into pale squares of sugarcane, into grey beaches where immense fishing nets were spread to dry. French fishermen seemed to pursue their prey in the same way as did Dominicans, lowering a long net between two canoes and throwing stones, or beating the sea with paddles to frighten the fish into it. As the stones splashed, little fountains rose to make rainbows. That was the year – 1935 – in which the volcanoes of Montserrat had been uncomfortably active, sending us earthquakes. I told the German how my husband and I – this was in our brief tourist period – had once walked from St Pierre to the foot of that grey scar on the mountainside which is nearly 3,000 feet high and, at close quarters, is seen to consist of grotesque boulders and flurries of ashes; a bare empty desolation seamed with chasms.

A facade of white uneven buildings outlined the bay of St Pierre. The German said: "Was it here the disaster? Of the ruins there are none to be seen." But I remembered paved streets lined by tumbled heaps of rubble; fragments of standing walls bound by creepers; sculptured fountains where lizards played. Thinking of the horror that happened in 1902, when the mountain split open its side and with one blast of its breath exterminated 30,000 people, I marvelled that men were willing to set up house again on the scene of the catastrophe. In my heart of hearts I have never quite believed in St Pierre. No West Indian town can ever have been so gay, so beautiful, so cosmopolitan as it is reputed to have been, now that it exists no longer. Only a few years ago I travelled with an old woman who remembered it well. She shrugged her shoulders at my questions; yes, it was pretty, with water flowing everywhere. At that time, aged 18, she had never seen any other city except Fort de France where she happened to be on that Ascension day of the disaster when 70 members of her family disappeared, including two brothers.

This was a golden timeless day. On the far horizon the Soufriere of St Vincent hung like a faintly purple shadow. The twin Pitons of St Lucia soared like two blue sugarloaves into the sky. HMS Diamond, a barren triangular rock from which in 1804, 120 British sailors defied the French fleet for 17 months, stood chalk white against the sea. Sometimes the little island gives so misty an impression that once I imagined that it was a ship on fire. Within half an hour of sunset our vessel swung into Castries, the capital of St Lucia and a port designed by the gods to be a perfect haven, but marred by men who had put on to every promontory yellow-brick barracks decorated with balconies.

In the middle of the harbour, insolent in her beauty, lay the flagship of the Atlantic fleet. Under the long grey guns slung from her turrets we could see little men in white uniforms, who wore golden chains on their breasts and gold stripes on their shoulders. As the sun set, the ensign was lowered and a bugle called. The sky flamed crimson, bathing sea and shore in the same colour; and it seemed as though the whole universe stood to attention while this far-flung fragment of the empire passed into darkness.

Inevitably, it was a sentimental moment and I said: "So beautiful a ship, and yet the thing she stands for is wrong."

And the German answered: "That is so. From now on it is not each other that we should fight but the love of all that," waving his hand in the direction of the warship, "which is in all of us." I took it that he was not an adherent of the rising menace called Hitler, but even so long ago one did not ask.

Our shabby little cargo boat crept unnoticed to her place by the wharf. Winches rattled all evening and sacks of flour were taken out of the hold and carried away on hand-carts. At midnight I felt the ship give a sudden lurch. Wrapped in a dressing gown I went on deck and watched huge waves, blue-black under the sky, billowing to the edge of the rail and then slipping under the ship's keel to dissolve in darkness. The newly risen moon touched with gold the line of white foam that was the last of St Lucia. Next morning I saw the sun rise behind the pale flatness that is Barbados.

I telephoned to Pat's school from the baggage warehouse and the headmistress invited me to stay for the two nights I was on the island. Pat was better in health, but I knew that she would never be happy in that place where she was not only a child from Dominica – a mud hole where people ate frogs – but also English and therefore doubly alien. In the following summer, we left her in England. In September of that year, Michael started school in Barbados where he remained, off and on, until he went to Cambridge. After saying goodbye to him, I waited at the bottom of the La

Haut hill for my horse and, sitting on a stone under a cocoa tree, heard with agony the farewell hooting of the ship that was taking my last child away.

In 1936, important things happened in Europe – Hitler's march into the Rhineland, the Spanish civil war, the abdication of the Prince of Wales. I remember it for our first return to Europe, for the publication of my first novel Duet in Discord, and for the birth of my first grandchild, Antony. Percy said over the telephone: "I'm afraid he's got my nose," with Margaret muttering in the background: "I never knew it to cramp your style, Boss," Margaret, who was nurse to both the Agar children, Antony and Elizabeth, deserves more than a passing mention. Like Cozier, she had deformed feet. Like Andrew Green she had the gift of memorable aphorisms. "Soap and water will wash away everything except sin," she said when the dog made a mess on the carpet. And again: "Cast your bread upon the waters and it will come back to you soaking wet!" "Prancing" was one of her favourite words: "Only to see the wood ants prancing by the telephone." It is a descriptive word, indicating pride and delight in movement. "The calves is prancing on the lawn" seems to mean more than little calves making mischief. All nannies of whatever colour have a special song or lullaby nostalgically remembered in after years. Margaret's was: "There is oil in your lamp, keep it burning. Keep it burning till judgment day." When Pat and Michael were babies, Nanny Pyle in Manchester used to sing: "Nor you nor me nor nobody knows, how oats, peas, beans and barley grows." Both these seem to open a metaphorically sad little window into the past.

On our visit to Europe in 1936, we coped with endless questions to which few people troubled to understand the answers. My mother-in-law, Lady Napier, gathered her grandchildren about her bed and said: "Now tell me all about Dominica." There could be nothing more dumb-making.

Pat tried, "Well, we have three beaches," and Lady Napier exclaimed: "But I never knew they grew in the tropics," thus creating a department of utter confusion.

"Where do you live as compared to Daphne?" I was asked, and began, "We live on the Atlantic side of the island," to be interrupted with, "And Daphne on the Pacific. I quite understand."

When we excused ourselves from playing tennis on the grounds of being out of practice, a charming American said, "Of course. It must be so difficult to play tennis on an island." Cross-examined on this surprising statement, she admitted she had visualised a coral atoll, with room on it for no more than a house and three palm trees, surrounded by greedy waves ready to engulf tennis balls. I still have a vulgar postcard sent from Antibes during the phoney war signed by Lorna Lindsley, Somerset Maugham, and Charlotte Boisevin whom I had known in Melbourne, which depicts exactly that sort of island. It is called Isle d'Amour, and shows a lady with advertisement teeth clasping a sailor in a pom-pommed beret who says, "The days would pass filled with the tenderest kisses" against a background of three rocks, two palm trees of assorted sizes, and one bamboo hut. People are appallingly vague about geography. When Michael was at Cambridge and referring to our life out here, a woman said to him, "It must be such fun to be able to pop over to Mexico for the weekend."

While we were staying with my aunt in France, the governess came down to dinner saying she had been listening to the radio. She told us that a curious thing had happened in Spain. A general of the army had flown over from the Canary Islands and started a war – it was, of course, the Spanish civil war.

Later, back in Dominica, Holly told me in a rare mood of self-deprecation that seldom in his life had he felt so strongly about anything as about Republican Spain, and yet he had done nothing, subscribed not a penny. I also had done nothing but talk.

In the previous year, the Italian assault on Abyssinia (now Ethiopia) had been a cause of bitter feeling among coloured peoples, and of discomfort to those of us who lived among them. The main road between Portsmouth and Marigot was being remade and oiled, and the coloured engineer in charge, who dined with us every Thursday, told us that the Abyssinian question had aroused racial feelings, which in Dominica were thought to be almost extinct. About a war in Africa there was passionate partisanship among these descendants of slaves on behalf of a country that unashamedly practised slavery. Logic is not more the prerogative of one race than of another. Labourers and drivers – a driver is an overseer of labour – inquired daily: "Will England interfere?" And when the answer was no, it was muttered up and down the road to the breaking of stones, "You can never trust a white man." And I believe serious trouble was averted only by the firm attitude of the coloured members of our legislature. Our engineer was himself trembling with rage and indignation against the British government, but we took it as a sign of friendship that the matter could be discussed at all.

The new road, which in point of fact was new only in a few places, had by that time reached Calibishie. What had been a red clay track became a grey and solid ribbon of macadam, here called "pitch". Coral had been torn from the sea, rocks and cliffs had been dynamited, oil for surfacing brought in drums from Trinidad. Men and women sat in the shade breaking stones, or "headed" them on wooden trays. As the road advanced – a benevolent dragon temporarily breathing fire and destruction – there was an ever-progressing stretch of car-racking, backbreaking, soul-shattering agony on the half-made road. Little shops sprang up, sponsored by Roseau and Portsmouth tradesmen, and these pursued the dragon from village to village and were welcomed by engineers and overseers who imagined that if men saw things they, or their women, desired, they were more likely to work for wages than to sit in the sun or go fishing.

One day, a man cutting coral found a fish stranded in a shallow pool and, having bludgeoned it to death, showed it to the driver. "I am going home," he said. "I have caught me a fish and so why should I work?" Which, to the driver, was a perfectly reasonable approach. The man had vegetables from his own garden and a "relish". What more could a man want? Tomorrow would be another day.

Holly's house at Hodges faced the trade winds from which he protected himself by two huge plate-glass windows. Beyond them was the glorious sweep of Woodford Hill bay with Hodges Island in the foreground where the white terns make their nests and a blowhole explodes its spray horizontally. Although, until the outbreak of war, he went back to the United States for his summers, Holly spent his winters here, occasionally playing tennis at the club in Roseau but more often just sitting, with a *pareu* wrapped about his loins, fretting about his houseboys, or dreaming up fabulous meals that never quite came off. A sudden cry of: "Oh, and Medly, a bayleaf," might be interpolated into a discussion on Mussolini or the dissection of a bridge problem.

It was continually surprising that in spite of his wide reading, his appreciation of good food, his delight in flower arrangements, Holly should have lived so uncomfortably, have been so aesthetically indifferent. Towards the end, he would not allow anything to be touched or tidied. (When I inherited his books, they had been gnawed by rats.) His was that curiously inverted form of snobbery that caused him to take less trouble rather than more to make a distinguished guest comfortable. When Somerset Maugham, who was an old friend from Tahiti days, and no longer in his first youth, came to stay with him no mosquito net was provided, and ants fell from the roof on to the bed. And when a friend came down the following week, he was told that he must sleep on the window seat because "When Maugham left we turned the mattress and found a nest of young snakes underneath. I have had to have it remade." No wonder that the novelist invited himself, with his secretary, to our guesthouse, which Pat and Michael celebrated with song:

Somerset Maugham
Sat on the lawn
He was all forlorn
And his pants were torn.

For which accusation, I may say, there was no justification whatever.

Another friend from Tahiti days was George Biddle, an American artist, who came with his fourth wife to stay with Holly at a time when his essential outhouse was incomplete. Helene was a sophisticated person, without desert-island mentality, but Holly offered her a roll of toilet paper and told her all Dominica was at her disposal. It was not surprising that she came over to see us most days although, being dependent on rainwater, we had no plugs to pull, but only little huts scattered about the garden. George complained that their host spent his days pondering upon what they should eat, and then it was scrambled eggs. We told him that in our day it had been "a little salad". When he returned to America, Biddle sent us each a drawing as a present. The Agars' one was of some really very peculiar figures preparing to enter the sea. When it was unpacked, Clifford asked, "Tell me, Sir, are they Christian people?" Two years later George was given a "profile" in the New Yorker, and became a member of the After Shave Club, which in those days signified celebrity. But he never came back to Dominica.

We had two resident artists of our own. One was Stephen Haweis of whom Gertrude Stein wrote in her book The Autobiography of Alice B Toklas: "Haweis was fascinated with what he had read of The Making of Americans. He did however plead for commas. Gertrude Stein said commas were unnecessary. However she liked Haweis very much and he had given her a delightful painting for a fan. She gave him two commas. It must be added, however, that on rereading the manuscript she took the commas out."

Stephen, who lived until his death in 1968 in the hills below Sylvania, with the greenest fingers of anyone I have known, had painted in Africa and the Pacific as well as the West Indies. My own favourites are his flower pieces and his fish. He was the first to say of our beaches, named black and white for the sand's texture: "I would never have believed that you would carry the colour question to such extremes."

We were surprised that as a painter he should turn his back on our enormous view and rather special sunset. Later, we discovered that he was of those who prefer the beauties of nature in miniature – a wild flower, a caterpillar, a leaf decayed to a tracery of veins. He once showed me a chrysalis that was like a piece of pale jade with a thin line of gold in it, and seven golden dots. Mounted on velvet in a Cartier's window, it would have caused a sensation.

The other artist was my son-in-law Percy Agar whose watercolours deserve to be better known outside the West Indies. In 1955, the year after he died, there was a successful exhibition of his work in Barbados. His studies of the roots of *mang* trees, of bamboos, of *rosinier* leaves are altogether enchanting. One of my favourites is a picture of the house

*The artist Stephen Haweis who lived in Dominica
until his death in 1968. As a young man he had
studied in Paris and known Gertrude Stein.*

Lennox built at the Chaudiere, backed by a huge *bois rivière*
with tree ferns and *balisiers* in the foreground. Besides being
a painter Percy was a distinguished naturalist, and James
Bond makes many acknowledgements to him in his book
Birds of the West Indies.

There are two parrots unique to Dominica, the smaller,
green *Amazona arausiaca* and the larger sisserou, *Amazona
imperialis*, and of a great rarity. Once I was lucky enough to
see a whole flock of them on the upper slopes of Morne
Diablotin, screaming in the early morning among immense
trees. A few years ago men from our village, camping below
the mountain, shot a sisserou for the pot and found inside its
body a fully formed egg on the point of being laid. "What

*Elma, Patricia,
and artist
Percy Agar, who
married Elma's
daughter Daphne.*

did you do with it?" my son-in-law cried in great excitement. "Why, Sir, we ate it." Hard boiled? Scrambled? Percy was too heartbroken to inquire.

This was after a not quite fully grown and totally uninjured specimen flew on to Percy's veranda and took up residence. It shared the family meals, insisting on a diet of bread and milk and cheese and egg; chewing a cotton reel or tweaking a belt, not deterred by the threat of: "Parrot pie tomorrow!" Green of back, purple of breast, sardonic of expression, refusing to be caressed, it remained to the end a bird of mystery, screaming, shouting, but enunciating for our comprehension not even so much as: "Nevermore." When Mr Polly died, apparently of heart failure after dive-bombing a domestic duck, the whole island mourned and absolutely nobody so much as thought of parrot pie.

The diablotin, Dominica's other speciality, now almost a legend, is generally considered to be extinct although a few enthusiasts still carry their hopes onto impregnable cliffs and mountains tops. A black-capped petrel, *Pterodroma hasitata*, this bird seems to have had something of the quality of the duck-billed platypus, both inspiring interest above the merit of their beauty. Père Labat, a French priest who spent time in Dominica, wrote in 1700: "The flesh of these birds is good and nourishing. It is only the difficulty of getting them which preserves the species ... They live on fish which they catch in the sea at night. They then return to the mountains where they live in holes like rabbits." While Thomas Atwood a hundred years later wrote: "The diablotin, so-called by the French for its uncommonly ugly appearance, is nearly the size of a duck and web-footed. The flesh is much admired by the French, who used formerly to export great numbers of them, salted; but the traffic was put an end to by the legislature of Dominica."

In the 1870s, the ornithologist Frederick Ober reported that the diablotin had not been seen for 50 years. But the ornithologist Sydney Porter, publishing as recently as 1930, wrote: "When making a journey through the forest my guide said there were still some diablotins upon the mountain; described them to me exactly, and said that their haunts were almost inaccessible." Since then there have been a few vague rumours – or a cry in the night. In the West Indies, as elsewhere, each man kills the thing he loves: dynamiting fish, exterminating game birds, shooting rare parrots. "For they eat good," said an old man whom I met prowling in the heights with his gun, "and when taught can speak as good as we."

In the dry season of 1934 when the *pois doux* was flowering, May the cook had died horribly by fire. Coming late to the preparation of dinner, she threw too much kerosene into the stove so that the sticks might easily be kindled, and the flames caught her dress. She rushed screaming into the sitting room where Lennox knocked her down and rolled her in a rug. But it was too late to save her, and two days later she died. So, in grief and terror, we learned that a negro's colour is only skin deep, and never to the ending of my life shall I forget the white patches on her body, surrounded by shrivelled skin curled up like the dead peelings you rub off after sunburn; nor the little red pattern of fire creeping over her hair like sparks burning off soot at the back of a chimney.

Then Alexa, who had "given a help" sometimes, came permanently into our service. Little butter-ball Alexa, so nicknamed by an American for her rounded figure and shining countenance, who could neither read nor write but who never forgot a recipe and could turn shilling and pence into dollars quicker than I could. One day I found a great girl in the kitchen and I asked: "Is that your daughter?" Thereupon Alexa covered her face with her hands and said: "Madame, she is my shame," surely an exaggerated gesture in a country where illegitimacy was reckoned at 70 percent. Years later, when her son married my house parlour maid, I asked her whether she was pleased about the engagement (my own son being newly married to my satisfaction), and she said: "Madame, what to do? I come old. Someone must look after him." Which had not been precisely my own reaction, but was after all a point of view.

Both Alexa's children were born out of wedlock, but late in life she married Felice, ex-smuggler and the best fisherman in the village; the same Felice who caught a shark way over by Marie Galante and, in seeking to take out the hook, stood on a thwart which broke, so that he fell into the mouth of the fish, who chewed his arm in its death throes. Other men made a tourniquet, and many hours later they came into Portsmouth where the newly arrived Polish doctor, who was more experienced in the brutalities of men than of fish, faced something he had not yet seen. He telephoned to me that never, never, would he have believed, but never... He was an excitable little man, prattling on and on to prepare us for death or amputation; but Felice walked out of hospital five days later with a patched-up limb that has served him well.

When she married, Alexa went to live in a large house near the sea, where her man's boat was beached under almond trees; and every morning and evening she walked the mile-long road through the village and up the hill to my kitchen, coping with a wood-burning stove and a coalpot. When, on their way from Jamaica, Princess Alice and the Earl of Athlone honoured my house by taking morning coffee on the veranda, Alexa pronounced as they drove away: "Madame, a pretty princess" as though we entertained ugly ones every day.

7 | A taste of colonial politics

It all began, our interest in local politics, while Lennox and I were tourists in the Caribbean in the spring of 1932, and had found the administrator of Dominica at loggerheads with most of the community. The Legislative Council, then consisting of two nominated and four elected members, had resigned en bloc because it refused to sanction increased taxation unless the salaries of English government officials were at the same time reduced. The late 1920s and the 1930s were lean years. The island suffered one hurricane after another. The value of her crops slumped in the world market. Limes, a principal source of revenue, were afflicted with diseases called red-root and wither tip. With copra at £9 a ton it was hardly worthwhile to pick up coconuts from the ground. But, being a grant-in-aid colony, unable to balance her own budget and the deficit being met from the imperial treasury, Dominica was not allowed to make her own economies, to cut her coat to a meagre cloth. He who pays the piper calls the tune. Seldom have the people of this curious, cantankerous island been so united. No candidates came forward to fill the vacancies on the Council. There were no elections. Posters carried the old and not particularly apposite slogan of the American colonies, No Taxation without Representation. Not for many months was the administrator able to persuade two white planters to accept nomination, thereby saving his face and that of His Majesty's government.

Following these appointments the new members were not only "cut in the clubs", but the house of one was burned to the ground and no one had any doubt that this was a political crime, although for all the evidence to the contrary the fire might have been started by a disgruntled servant. "Burned to the ground" is the cliche, but actually the charred walls still stand among sad trees, and one can imagine those stealthy figures carrying petrol and *flambeaux*. Fire is not only a menace in the West Indies but a weapon. Probably there is more arson than is ever admitted. In my time there have been three serious fires in Roseau, and many of the sites remain empty, making the once pretty little town resemble a mouth with missing teeth.

In 1932, while we were still negotiating for our property, Lennox made the acquaintance of two of the intransigent politicians, and on his return to London he interviewed, at their request, Sir Robert Hamilton, the parliamentary secretary to the Colonial Office, and explained their grievance. Sir Robert received my husband sympathetically and, although nothing whatever was achieved, after all to reduce the salary of an official would be quite unthinkable,

Lennox acquired great kudos in the island.

These storms in tea cups which, in the past 20 years, have swollen like little drops of water into mighty oceans, do not interest the mother country in the way they interest those who live in the far-flung outposts. There have been so many outposts, and now they grow beautifully less. Squabbles in legislative councils look rather petty from the metropolis – or at least petty enough to be ignored. It took the Colonial Office a long time to shift the telescope from the blind eye. Yet these tempests are, in miniature, precisely those which rend mighty nations. The unimportance of an individual does not lessen his toothache while the smallness of an island does not reduce its grievance. Regrettably it is only by noise that one can make oneself felt. To get one's way one must have a nuisance value.

Largely as the result of the sound and fury in 1932, a new constitution was granted to Dominica in 1937, this time with five elected members instead of four. The elected and mainly coloured element was increased to form a majority over the officials and nominated members. At this time, a "sugar baron" from Antigua wrote to a mutual friend in England: "Tell your pal on the windward coast of Dominica to get out while the going is good. They would be safer in Liberia."

Already one section of the community, confronted with this first groping movement towards self-government was asking: "What guarantee has a black people that black aristocrats will govern them less selfishly than white aristocrats?" To which there can be no answer except: "None." A point that the liberal Englishman does not

*Lennox Napier (back row, second left) with other
members of the Legislative Council, 1937.*

always understand, believing that to put a black man in
power favours the underdog.

Lennox, although regarded presumably as a white
aristocrat, was received at public meetings with speeches
and feasting. Asked to stand as an elected member of the
North Eastern district, in 1937 he was elected unopposed
and, until his death, he represented the parishes of St
Andrew and St David (in the former of which we resided) in
the Legislative Council. It was a long thin district, wide only
from the mountains to the sea but extending from the
extreme north, where the island might have been sliced with
a knife, so unbroken and impassive are those smooth-faced
cliffs, to the Ouanary River at La Plaine in the south-east
where ragged black cedars line the beach and the tide swirls
with a savage undertow along a coast from which for weeks
at a time it is impossible to launch a boat.

The then administrator was not best pleased that Lennox

was now a member of the legislature saying to my husband's sponsors, "I suppose that now he will be going to the secretary of state behind my back." And indeed, in the following year, 1938, he went, not behind anybody's back but with everybody's approval, to consult with Malcolm Macdonald, the then secretary of state for the colonies, about many matters which concern a small island – its peasant agriculture, soil erosion and road development. So it was that Lennox was to give the last of his health, on his last visit to England, to Dominica's affairs.

That same year, while the rape of Austria was being accomplished in Europe and our potential allies flung one after another to the wolves, we visited in the way of Lennox's duty the extreme north of the island. There we stayed the night at an old house called Reposoir where, at the very edge of a 500 feet cliff, and so lost in scrub that trees grew out of graves, there was a burying place where slaves lay on one side of the path and white people on the other. Beyond it was an overhanging rock from which you might look down into the Atlantic Ocean. My son Michael said: "What a grand place for executions." But I thought how grateful suicides would be for the chance of so beautiful and clean a death: the sea blue, and white horses flecking it. At that time, one read of Jewish women forced to clean lavatories in their fur coats, or scrub pavements in their chemises.

We had come to this place on account of a crane. At the foot of the cliff there was an estuary where water squirmed over boulders squared by the hand of God. From a flat shelf, washed lightly by the swell, rafts could be set afloat, or even boats. Beyond the stream a low excrescence of rock jutted into the sea to make a natural breakwater to leeward of which was only swell and not, as elsewhere, crashing impossible waves. The manager, a small and nut-brown American, said that if a crane were erected bananas could be safely lowered into a launch and a whole district opened to cultivation.

"But how would you transport your fruit?" we asked, for the path down which we had slid on grey dust and stones was not for donkeys.

"Give me a crane," said the American, "and I'll give you a track. For a little food and a little rum the people will make one. It is nothing to them to carry a bunch of figs this way. Give me a crane and there is a future for Reposoir."

An old crane was available from the Roseau jetty, which, a year or so previously, had been rammed by a steamer. (The bridge had telegraphed: "Full astern," and the engineer had given her "full ahead", the sort of mistake that might happen to anyone.) Now the government was standing us not only a new jetty but also a new crane. So it was thought that the old one would look well here, cemented into a God-made jetty that no steamer could crumple and no waves batter down. So Lennox promised to recommend its erection. I even believe that it was done. But I have never been back to that place, and although the motor road is creeping nearer I doubt if I ever shall.

We had met the American 18 months before. On December 10 1936, we had been sitting in the coastal launch waiting to leave for Roseau. Mailbags had been thrown on board and one rope already cast off, when a fellow passenger was called to the telephone. In what appeared to be three of his long-legged strides he reached the little tin building housing the exchange. When he joined us again he was bareheaded: "Ladies and gentlemen," he said very gravely, "His Majesty the King has abdicated." Silently and reverently we acknowledged the not unexpected information, standing as it were by a deathbed. And the American, who was a stranger to us, looked up in a bewildered way and said: "What king?" Dominica had been as passionately interested as the rest of the world in the story of a king's love for the divorced Mrs Wallis Simpson. For three days the island had been about its business on tiptoe. Without benefit of written word the news spread by sea and forest path to the uttermost villages; was borne on the wings of fishing boats and whispered in rum shops and on crowded lorries. "That lady has given our king a tea." You may drink "bush tea" for almost anything. Infusions of grass or leaves or bark may cure fever, headache, and indigestion. But this was supposed to be a love potion, a drop of something essentially feminine, secretly put into the cup. They say that if you do this, your man will never stop loving you.

"Why, it was this way," the American explained when we found him again at Reposoir. "I've never taken out a subscription, not even to local nooz. I was waiting to see how I got fixed. Now if I had had a radio ..."

The wooden house had faded to grey under the sea wind. Sunshine pierced the cracks between boards and fell on to floors rotted by insect and rain. A few crooked shelves held pots and pans and tumblers, a looking-glass, old magazines – "New if you haven't read them," said the American.

There, off the coast at the Reposoir estate where the Caribbean met the Atlantic, wind and current made a thin line of foam as though a seine net had been dragged across the channel to trace the boundary between two seas. "My mother-in-law," said the American, "could remember when it was a common thing to sail over to Marie Galante for mass, and for Frenchmen coming to Reposoir to dance the weekend through."

The American's mother-in-law was a legendary figure: one of the matriarchs spewed up by the Victorian age out of the subjection of women. Widowed, and her sons dead, she had managed the estate alone, and built drying sheds for cocoa purposely to shut out the sight of the sea. "She could not make a house pretty," said the American. "She had no use for a view. She cared only for the land." And at last she lay bedridden, bullying servants and sons-in-law, with the land failing through no fault of her own, and the people pilfering from under the very bed she lay in. "This is God's truth," he said, "that a man came in one night to steal cocoa, and the old lady having heard him, cried out, so that he fled, dropping his hat, and walked in next morning to claim it, saying that the wind must have blown it to Reposoir."

But it seemed that the old lady was not allowed to die in that bed, for it is the tragedy of the old that they may not die where they please, but are harried for their own good to where it is least trouble to keep them.

"After the hurricane," said the American, "the boat was mashed up; heads were torn off coconuts; cocoa lay on the ground. We couldn't leave her alone here, with only servants." So she, a free-born coloured lady who had chosen her last resting place – her final Reposoir – in the old graveyard on the cliff's edge, and who would have lain not on the slaves' side but among white people, was taken to Roseau to die in a dusty street where motorcars were heard, and children playing scales, and hard shoes tapping the pavement. And was buried with the pomp and circumstance of a first-class funeral, among crosses and headstones.

The American had taken down the drying sheds which impeded the view of the French islands for he felt that if a man could see smoke rising, even 20 miles away, and towns shining in the sunset, he was not so lonely as he might otherwise be. Purple bougainvillea broke the sharpness of the cliff's edge; the heads of coconut palms had sprouted again. "But," he said, refilling our punch glasses, "it is hard to get a jelly-nut for my own use because the people still pilfer. They don't reckon it stealing to take a nut or a fig from the old estate. It is as though it were still our business to feed them."

We went to Europe a few weeks later, to meet our own troubles. For this was the last expedition that Lennox and I were ever to make together, our last "explore" and by the time we came back there was a depression in bananas and Lennox was very ill with TB.

At first, however, it seemed as though we had picked up

Lennox, who died in 1940, with Elma in England, 1936.

the pieces. Entering the house we had made together in happiness, I took hold of Lennox's hand and said: "It's all right, isn't it?"

And he answered: "It's all right."

At our feet surf was breaking over rocks and islands. Spray from the blowhole hung motionless as a cloud. The air was full of the sweet scent of stephanotis, of the call of doves. For a little while it was as though nothing had changed. We saw the moon set in the dawn, spreading a golden radiance over the sea; and when the kingfisher rattled a greeting and sunlight caught its feathered throat it glistened like silk. The people of the village came up in ones and twos to see the master. Bedneau said: "Of course we must all love Jesus, but after Jesus we love you, Sir and Madame."

Lennox attended one or two more meetings of the Legislative Council but he did not go to the beach any more. He had been told that he must not lie in the sun. Once or twice I saw him watching us from a clearing at the top of the cliff, which we call the "look out". Below it, the face of the rock is carved by rain into runnels, as a human face might be wrinkled with tears. Here are scrubby palms bearing a golden inedible fruit, and white orchids sprouting from the ground or lodged in the branches of trees. From the look out one has a view of the bathing pool scoured out between sand and rocky islet, and we are able to distinguish as from nowhere else where is deep water and where reef. Beyond the beach one looks to a red promontory shaped like a lion couchant; and again to a grey headland pierced at the end as by the eye of a giant needle.

Lennox had been especially forbidden to wade in rivers. A chair was constructed by which he might be carried to the Chaudiere. And it was there that we faced together the fact that he was not cured, and that he never would be. Quite suddenly he lost his voice altogether and could do no more than mouth his words. I went for a little walk by myself, up river above the Chaudron where the stream is dark and tempestuous under trees, and back through the rough pasture where there are clumps of breadfruit seedlings; and crossed the river again where it ran smooth and quietly under a huge fig. I never to this day see that place without remembering.

Next day from Pointe Baptiste I telephoned the doctor, and he said: "You know that the second lung has gone." I had not known it was affected.

One day a man came to borrow 300 dollars, for what specific purpose I cannot remember. He took no offence when he was refused but told us that Lennox should drink a cabbage palm tea. "You must go to the tree at sunrise and at sunset and say, 'Tree, I come.' And then slash off bark on each side three times and afterwards make a tea and drink it every day for nine days." A sailor in the little back parlour of a shop in Portsmouth had already told me that my husband would recover if he ate only crapaud soup and drank champagne. Women said to me: "When we hear the Master is sick, we cry, cry, cry, but what to do?" Meaning, there was nothing to do.

The invasion of Poland by the Nazis made background to our misery as in the previous year had Hitler's annexation of the Sudetenland. The names were different but the situation was the same. Late in August I had been to Roseau – there was still no through road to the capital; as usual, we travelled by launch and bus. On the way home the driver told me: "Russians and Germans have made a pact."

"Oh, Leonard," I said, "I don't believe it. You've got it wrong."

In that year there was a bamboo flowering quite close to the road. A bamboo flowers about once in 50 years, which hardly anyone had seen. Leonard-of-the-bus was running excursions. I looked at the feathery tufts of brown and beige and blossom and repeated over and over: "It isn't true."

With the rest of the world we havered: "Do we? Do we not?" as one might play she-loves-me-she-loves-me-not with daisy petals. Very early in the morning of September the third, four hours by the sun before the news was known in Europe, the wife of the crown attorney telephoned to say that we were at war.

8 | War and death

On that day in 1939 when the Germans marched into Poland, our defence force, all 30 strong of it, went into the barracks on Morne Bruce, taking up quarters in those old four-square buildings with roofs rusted to the colour of mango flowers. The governor proclaimed that the island would be defended to the last man, and to the last – the only – gun. The administration bombarded us with special gazettes. Defence of the Realm acts littered the streets. To facilitate machine-gun practice a lovely saman tree was cut down at the corner above the Roseau post office where the market overflowed on to the sea front and where, on a Saturday, you might bestride trays of eggplants and tomatoes, with pumpkins and pawpaw and red peppers, and be interpellated by women who cry, "Madame, you not wanting cauliflowers?" or "Madame, pineapple for you?"

There was a nightly blackout ordered of all streets and windows facing the sea so that only the blazing electricity of

Government House and the red lights, one on the jetty and the other on the old grey fort which is used as police headquarters, guided friendly or enemy shipping into the roadstead. When a steamer stayed overnight, passengers sweltered in cabins and saloons behind darkened and sealed ports while gangway and hatches were floodlit to permit the working of cargo.

Trade was for a few days altogether dislocated. It seemed that our money was no longer our own although not yet definitely belonging to any one else. A committee appointed to consider food prices showed bias in favour of the consumer, and from all over the island rose the wailing of merchants. There was created that somehow risible title, the Competent Authority.

The administrator pronounced: "There can and I trust there will be no profiteering in our midst at a time of crisis."

"War profiteering, indeed," cried Mr Pentecost from his long low shop where nails and corned beef and kerosene and rolls of "cloth" (which is the word for cotton goods) were inextricably jumbled; and where hens picked a living off the floor and from between the hard soil-stained toes of customers; and where much rum was drunk of an evening and many strange things spoken. "There is no profit at all. They make me sell at the price I buy. The freight from town I can pay out of my losings."

Admittedly there was hardship. A country shopkeeper could not afford to sell at Roseau prices when he must pay for the launch, for the bus, for porterage. With each transfer a little profit slipped inevitably from one set of fingers to another. Shops were closed in protest and I telephoned to the administrator: "Sir, the storekeepers are raising a riot."

"How many storekeepers?"

"Two."

"Ah, well," he said in a soothing voice, "it takes three, technically, to make a riot."

And our village carpenter told me that Mr Pentecost, who used to sell for one-and-a-penny hinges that cost ninepence in Roseau, had now put the price of these up to one-and-eight pence as a war emergency.

"And I think", said the carpenter, "that he will not sell the hinges before the rust has them in powder."

Mr Pentecost had other troubles that season. A discarded mistress had in revenge thrown his account books down the privy.

"Even," he wailed to me, "I send her child to school in 'tennis'." To go to school in tennis shoes, what we used to call sandshoes or plimsolls, carried prestige; and almost certainly the "tennis" were carried, and put on at the door, as were Sunday-go-to-meeting shoes borne on a man's head above his hat.

In October a strange craft was sighted on the leeward coast, a boat with no beginning and no end, bow indistinguishable from stern as though a beige whale had been half submerged; and this creature hugged the shore, the panting of its hit-and-miss engine echoing up valleys and among mountains. It was debated whether this were one of Hitler's secret weapons, a submarine, like the crocodile in Peter Pan, which had swallowed a clock. The commanding officer of the defence force knew that the territorial waters of Dominica should not be violated by persons unknown.

The craft must be intercepted, although there were only rowing boats with which to intercept. Remembering, however, that on Mondays the motor launch Hope ploughed its weary way from Portsmouth to Roseau, he met her at Massacre, boarded by canoe, and commandeered her in the name of the king.

Only a few weeks previously someone had asked the engineer-captain of the Hope: "What will you do in the Great War?" And as he wriggled with embarrassment, I had said: "What better could he do than command the navy of Dominica?" Now here was the navy going into action; overloaded; cluttered with women and children.

"It is hysterical madness," jabbered Mr Pentecost, "to take a civilian population into such danger."

"Furthermore," pronounced Holly, who was on board that day, with all the sangfroid of a neutral citizen, "it is nearly lunch-time. I propose that the passengers be landed so that I can telephone for a car."

Precious minutes would be wasted, but on the other hand civilians must be protected. Eventually, first-class passengers drove into town and second-class ones sat on the shingle under the church, listening to the slow drag of waves on rounded stones, watching a man reset a fish pot, and sighing a little over the eccentricities of the white man's war. It was being said in our village: "England and France talk a great deal about fighting, but it seems that they do not fight."

The crocodile with a clock turned out to be a ferryboat on its way from New York to Brazil, rolling down to Rio (emphasis on the rolling) to ply in that stupendous harbour. I doubt whether in all history there can have been a more unpleasant voyage. How the bar was stocked I do not know, but we understood that during their brief stay, the Brazilians were hospitable to our navy and the defence force. A good time was had by all until the launch captain remembered to go back for the second-class passengers still sitting on the beach, bringing them into Roseau an hour and a half behind schedule. There was no ill-feeling about this. What is any more or less to the patience of Dominicans?

Quite soon the government decided it could no longer afford to keep the defence force in barracks. Our brave boys returned to business as usual. The moon rose behind the waterfalls in the Roseau valley unremarked by any save lovers and the headless drummer. We were left, as a local editor put it, at the mercy of anyone.

At the end of the month, a threat of hurricane made everybody forget the war. For two days in succession the glass fell two tenths at evening, and on the third day it was equally low at dawn. Mountains stood up bleakly against the sky, their valleys traced by purple scars while the summit of the Soufriere mountain in Guadeloupe, 50 miles away, seemed to hang in mid air, its base swathed in a white mist. So calm was the sea that the reef showed itself purple under the green water, and one could distinguish between patches of sand and dark caverns.

Suddenly a school of porpoises came into the bay. These creatures, often cavorted by the side of a launch, expressing the perfect poetry of motion as their sleek bodies dived and rose again without effort, but this was the only time I ever saw them from the veranda. So unexpectedly did the grey shapes appear out of nowhere that for a moment we breathed: "Submarines!" until the sea was filled with more porpoises than Germany could have mustered in U-boats. So unnatural was the stillness that I found myself talking too loudly, forgetting that there was no longer need to shout against the sound of the waves which is normally so much part of my life that, like the night-time shrilling of crickets, it is no longer noticed.

On the third day the wind rose from the north, blowing rain horizontally into the house. Water poured through closed jalousies as though forced from below, streaming under doors. Hurricane shutters were fastened, and wedges and hammer produced to tighten the bars. The trap door into the basement was tested and food made easily available. Orange rivers poured from the gullies in the cliffs to spread their stain far beyond the limits of the bay; while out of a flat sea heavy sullen waves broke in an orange foam. But already we had been notified by telephone that the storm had passed Dominica by. It was a phoney hurricane, like the phoney war.

In the afternoon, rain and wind having abated, I went down into the village. But for the trickling of water the world was quiet. Miniature cascades poured from every gully. Where gutters had been choked by landslides deposits of red mud lay on the road, and there were pools of water filled with dead insects. Frail wooden houses still kept their eyes closed as though they were asleep. And I wondered what people did in such weather. Had they an infinite capacity for slumber? Did they pick fleas from their dogs or lice from each other, or plait and replait their hair into complicated patterns?

There was a banana tree fallen in the street which the publican was trying to remove. "Too much of wind," he said shaking his head, "too much of rain." Then he told me that a cow had been carried out to sea. His wife, standing in the doorway of her house, asked me. "Madame, if war reach to Dominica, will it be worse than hurricane?"

Pat had come out to the West Indies for her summer holidays and we did not send her back to England. For the next three years she was at school in Antigua, while Michael returned to school in Barbados at the end of September 1939. Lennox lived through the winter, failing visibly from day to day, swallowing nothing but liquids and only with great pain. When imminent sentence of death was passed he said, although not yet 49, "I have had a good life."

When his retirement from the Legislative Council had become inevitable, a petition was signed by his 300 or so voters requesting me to take his place. I was returned unopposed in February 1940, confident that Lennox's friends would stand by me, and that for a little while he would be there to instruct and guide. "If Mrs Napier is elected," he wrote in his farewell message to his constituents, "there will be continuity of policy, and I shall be able as before to give your interests my personal consideration." But he died two weeks later; and then the Tribune newspaper ran a great headline: "Dominica mourns the death of Mr Napier."

At the next meeting of Council the senior member cried: "I say without fear of contradiction that he has given of his very best to the interests of the island and the welfare of his people. To this Council his loss is irreparable."

Lennox's last whisper was: "Thank you for all that you have done for me". Which was a nice thing to have had by me, through the years. He died in the early morning and I waited until dawn before calling the servants. "The Master dead?" Louisa said. "Dead since we saw him last night?" As soon as the telephone exchange opened at seven o'clock I began telephoning.

He was buried that afternoon in his own ground in a place of his own choosing, for he hated the idea of a graveyard, although country cemeteries in Dominica are the prettiest I have seen anywhere: not too well tended, the little wooden crosses half hidden by a kind of croton called redbush, and a yellow smothering of alamanda. Often graves are decorated with empty conches, those shells with tender pink linings that are used as trumpets to announce the killing of a cattle or a catch of fish. Are they so placed, I wonder, that the angels may use them on the day of judgement?

All day the people of the village gathered round, bringing flowers to the house. His bed was heaped with roses and hibiscus, with red lilies and white orchids and little tight bunches of daisies and carnations. All day Bryant made a coffin and Freddie dug a grave. Launches and buses brought down the administrator and my husband's colleagues. The people who had worked for him carried his coffin. An English neighbour read a few prayers by the graveside. By five o'clock everybody had gone away, and Daphne and I were left alone.

Holly Knapp died suddenly a month later, and I buried him beside my husband in that quiet place under trees, within sound of the sea. He had dined with me the night before, and next morning Medly came crying that he had found his master dead in his bed. "It is not true", said Louisa. "I not troubling Madame with a story like that." But it was true, and for the second time within four weeks I must order a coffin and prepare a grave.

So these two, who had met 20 years before in Tahiti, lay side by side in a little clearing among palms and frangipanis. On a tall and strong tree I put a bee orchid, carrying four-foot long yellow and brown whips of blossom, which I had found on a ridge high above the Chaudiere. The village carpenter made headstones and six-inch-high walls with small pieces of coral enclosing what were meant to be rectangular spaces for flowers. But land crabs lodged in the coral and ate everything we planted except the common white orchid which clings indiscriminately to wood or stone.

Through time unreckoned
Lay this brown earth for him. Now is he come.
Truly he hath a sweet bed.

Two days after Holly's death, the Germans attacked Norway and the phoney war was over. It was my instinct to run over and tell him, but never again would I travel, with telephone message or newspaper, that dark path through second-growth forest in which remained here and there primitive giants, old gnarled trees wound about with the roots of parasites which resembled thread on a spool.

I tried and failed to sell Holly's house as it stood. "I do not want a house there," said the owner of the land, "and if I did I would not want that house." Within a year the people were filching here a nail and there a hinge, and so we dismantled it, selling boards and fittings and sending the proceeds to Holly's sister in America. Soon, at Holly's place, it was possible to know where a house had been only because the trees were less high than those surrounding what had once been a clearing.

The days of Dunkirk, foggy in the English Channel, were hazy in Dominica also and the French islands were hidden. Marie Galante was no more than a faint flat line on the horizon and Guadeloupe – which by tricks of sunlight I have seen pale blue and indigo, pink and purple and even gold – was altogether invisible. We knew nothing of what was happening over there, except that men were *mobilisés*. Our people thought that we also should be conscripted. Times were hard, and army pay worth coveting. In September 1939, 100 men had volunteered but they had not yet been called up. Coloured people were slightly on their dignity, insisting that their boys should be regular soldiers and not thrust into labour battalions as had happened in the first world war. A rumour percolated that Hitler had bargained this should be a white war.

"Why object to that?" I said. "The sooner we exterminate each other the sooner the world will be yours.

On Empire Day, May 24, I gave away certificates instead of prizes at the school sports in Marigot. Some elderly gentlemen had said it was not decent that little boys should run about in the sun while men were dying by thousands in Europe, but I felt that if we yielded to that spirit we should no longer order a meal or write a letter or plant pumpkins. It was decided to hold the sports, but that the winners should donate their prize money to the Red Cross, receiving instead an acknowledgment of prowess. I never heard what the children themselves thought; whether they felt themselves compensated for the tops and penknives distributed in other villages by a "paper" endorsed by my signature.

The sports ground was a long way from the main road. There are not many such flat places in Dominica. It was as though the hill had had its top sliced off like a boiled egg. We could see there was a breeze blowing, but under a shelter of canvas and palm branches, which constituted the grandstand, it was unbearably hot. Glare off the beaten ground made my head ache. Over and over I wrote my name on squares of paper destined to be pasted on wooden walls among advertisement calendars and pictures of Our Lady. Flat race, boys under twelve. Threading the needle race, girls over twelve. High jump. Donkey race. Tug of war. Never before or since has my autograph been so strenuously sought after.

The schoolmaster, short and black; the Methodist minister, tall and white; the store keeper, the estate overseer, all immaculate in starched suits which miraculously had not wilted, were out on the field organising, time-keeping, measuring. Little boys and girls ran about in the sun while in Europe men and women and children were smashed to

Elma Napier, the only woman in Dominica's Legislative Council in 1949. She first sat on the Council in 1940.

pieces; or, as refugees, crowded the congested roadways.

When the sports were over the schoolmaster thanked me for coming, and I thanked the schoolmaster for thanking me. I congratulated the winners on winning; congratulated everyone on the fine spirit shown.

"Not even those of us," I said, "who can remember the worst moments of the last war," tears had been threatening all day and my voice shook a little, "not even we have known the Empire to be in such danger as now."

We had heard that morning that the Germans had taken Boulogne. I had crossed the Channel two days before Chamberlain went to Munich to bring back "peace in our time". The train had pulled out with drawn blinds. Now I wondered when, if ever, a French train would steam out of Boulogne again.

The children to whom I had handed out scraps of paper had never heard of Boulogne nor seen a train. When it was all over we went down to the ramshackle store by the bay side to listen to the six o'clock news. The space outside was packed with black faces, hearing the voice of England. One did not know how much they understood; whether they were frightened. The smooth refined BBC voice was not really telling us anything.

"Some day," I surmised to the old Englishman who was still living by charity in the slave quarters of an estate house near the village, "some Gibbon will be writing the Decline and Fall of the British Empire."

And the major answered: "I wonder where he will begin."

The old man had recently envisaged a series of educative talks to the Caribs, but he had never got further than the opening words of the first one. "The two most important things in life," he began, "are food and sex." Black eyes, bright and round as beads sewn on to the faces of toy dogs, registered faint bewilderment. A copper-coloured woman nervously twisted her long hair. "Food and sex," he repeated, at which psychological moment a shell was blown to announce that fish had been caught, whereupon the whole audience scampered down hill to the beach, for now the only important thing in life was fish. And the would-be lecturer was left alone with the magistrate and two policemen.

The major had written a poem in memory of my husband, which he entitled Death and Rebirth. "Death is a myth, a sacrificial strife evoked through ignorance, an evil spell...." I could never myself pretend fully to understand the major's sonnets to which, on suitable occasions he would affix such titles as "epithalamium", or "epicedium". And there was a most unfortunate contretemps when a local paper, having accepted a contribution dedicated to Plotinus, misprinted the dedication as to Pretonlus, who was not at all the same person.

On the day Paris surrendered, I was alone at Pointe Baptiste. The sea was streaked with purple shadows; slow lazy waves broke onto the rocks. My big flamboyant tree was alive with hummingbirds. I looked over to the islands called the Saints – pyramids to the sphinx of Guadeloupe – where, in 1782, Admiral Rodney had defeated the French fleet, and I was glad that Lennox had not had to endure the fall of France, a country which he so much loved.

After the fall of France to the Germans, the "sugar barons" of Guadeloupe and Martinique threw in their lot with Marshal Pétain under the dictatorship of Admiral Georges Robert. A curtain of silent hostility fell between the French and British islands. Only the little fishing boats, the smugglers, retained their neutrality, their freedom of entry on either side of the channel.

Once I asked a woman from Marie Galante whether it was true that German submarines were refitting over there, and she said: "*Mais, Madame, presque jusqu'aux quais.*" It is to my regret that I have never set foot on Marie Galante, that low island on my right, although I know intimately the shadowed valleys between cane fields, the white estate houses, the town which, of late years, has been so brilliantly illumined at night. The northern promontory is so close to sea level that a factory chimney appears to rise straight out of the ocean like a slim pencil; and sometimes, when there is burning of cane refuse, black smoke rolls over the sea.

In the first summer of the war, an English schoolmaster from Barbados came to Dominica for his holidays, a man so pacifist in his views that he refused even to subscribe to Red Cross funds. For the sake of adventure he slipped over to Marie Galante and was immediately thrown into prison. Through secret Carib contacts, this became known and he was expensively ransomed it being certain that had the very anti-British governor of Guadeloupe arrived in time for his trial he would have been interned for the duration, or even more unpleasantly dealt with. This experience made such a psychological impression that the schoolmaster straightway resigned from pedagogy and joined the British navy.

In 1808, Marie Galante was for a little while in English hands, and a naval medical officer has left a record of life under an occupation to which the French seem to have submitted gracefully. Their method of dealing with the invaders was to supply the marines liberally with rum. "The invasion had taken place in early spring; by May the men began to suffer from ulcers; in June they were dying of fever within 24 hours; at the beginning of August the officers succumbed and eight died within a fortnight. The garrison was reduced to 200 men of whom one hundred and 60 were in hospital." It was not so absurd to suppose that this method of waging war should have been repeated in the 1940s, when contraband between us and the Vichy-controlled islands was so much part of our everyday life that one almost took it for granted. One evening I was entertaining two senior officials on my veranda and, seeing a foreign-rigged vessel making for Calibishie, I said without thinking, "There's the French mail coming in." Only by shifting their chairs so that they had their backs to the sea and by totally ignoring the remark did my guests acknowledge my manque de tact. The last thing they wanted brought to their notice was the completely illegal "French mail".

9 | "Must I wear a hat?"

It was with considerable trepidation that I attended my first meeting of the Legislative Council's finance committee. "Must I wear a hat?" I asked the administrator the night before. This was the first time that a woman had broken into the sacred places. There were no precedents, no protocols; no one cared whether I wore a hat or not. Finance committee had obviously been instituted for the consideration of the island's finances but in my time it had come to mean a meeting of the whole council for the discussion of everything. The public was not admitted: one might smoke, interrupt, ignore the agenda. As a friendly way of talking shop it was far more satisfactory than a formal meeting of the legislature.

My first finance committee meeting coincided with the inter-Windward Island cricket tournament for the Cork Cup. On January 1 1940, Dominica, for various complicated and forgotten reasons, had ceased to be a

Leeward island and became one of the Windward group. At the last moment there was sudden passionate objection to this new "selling into slavery". But when the Dominica cricket team was paid the compliment of being invited to compete for the Cork Cup, public opinion swung round wholeheartedly in favour of the change. Cricket easily prevailed where reason had failed to convince. In those days, when a Test match was being played anywhere in the world, the mayor of Roseau would make formal application that the electricity which normally functioned only between dusk and midnight be allowed to run all day so that persons might listen to the wireless. Crowds would gather in the streets outside any house where there was a loudspeaker. When a match was actually taking place in the island, shops and offices would close for the day so that everybody might be free to watch the game played on that lovely lawn surrounded by saman trees in the Botanical Gardens.

Dominica has always, cricket apart, been remarkable for the number of its bank holidays. Andrew Green said: "In Roseau every day is a holiday except Thursday, which is a half holiday." All through that first committee meeting members were wriggling to be away. If a councillor spoke at any length, his honour would turn to the clock behind him and say: "Gentlemen, we shall miss the first over." When he, in turn, addressed the meeting, members would ostentatiously crook elbows to consult wristwatches. Hitherto I had had the piety of a neophyte, but never since that morning have I taken unduly seriously the pompous deliberations of men. Eventually our discussion was adjourned until the following day, and thus I was detained for an extra 24 hours in Roseau. What could I do but watch cricket?

No meeting of the Legislative Council was summoned for several months. According to the constitution there had to be at least one meeting every year; and our then administrator was so afraid of us or so bored that he very nearly abided by the letter of the law. It is written in the minutes: "The oath of allegiance was administered to Mrs Elma Napier", wording which lends something of a medical flavour to the bald statement, the suggestion of a nauseous draught forcibly swallowed. "I Elma Napier, do swear that I will be faithful and bear true allegiance to His Majesty King George the Sixth, his heirs and successors according to law. So help me God." The oath for the Executive Council, composed of the most important members of the Legislative Council and on which I once served for a few months, was far more portentous, including the promise of secrecy.

The Legislative Council members sat at a long table covered with blue baize, the five elected members on the left, three nominated members and two officials on the right. There was at that time no question of party government. One administrator always referred to us five elected members en bloc as His Majesty's loyal opposition, and indeed we were generally against the government, sitting to criticise, to clamour, to pass with amendments bills drafted by the crown attorney. Often we differed passionately among ourselves but basically we were on the same team. And I think that for a small and poverty-stricken island it was better so.

Sun poured through the window behind the throne upon

which sat the administrator. In front of him lay the silver mace presented to the colony by Sir William Young who was governor in the 1770s. A slight breeze would ruffle the tattered colours of the royal regiment of Dominica, long since disbanded. Four glass-fronted bookcases stuffily sheltered our law library. Proceedings opened with prayer. The minutes of the last meeting, having been circulated, were taken as read and confirmed.

On one occasion, the crown attorney gave notice of his intention to move at a later stage the first reading of 18 bills. The acting treasurer gave notice of his intention to move at a later stage the first reading of three bills and five resolutions. Actually, it was customary for bills to pass through all stages at one sitting. Then, on the second reading, the crown attorney moved "that the House resolve itself into committee to consider the bill clause by clause," whereupon the clerk of the council would swing the mace over his head and formal rules were suspended, members talking in turn or out of it, and even interrupting each other.

I remember one crown attorney, suffering from a hangover, being totally unable to enunciate the required formula. "I beg to move," he began, and came to a dead stop. On the second try he came to: "I beg to move that the House..."

"Yes, Mr Crown Attorney," said the administrator encouragingly, "try just once more." At last it all came out in a mad rush, as though the sentence had been one long incomprehensible word. Someone suggested that what we really needed was a gramophone to make the crown attorney's motions and a crane to swing the mace.

My first Legislative Council dinner – normally these happened during the budget session – took place at the next visit of Sir Henry Popham, the governor of the Windward Islands. His Excellency had, on that occasion, included heads of departments – agriculture, public works, education, medicine, what-have-you. I was the only woman among 19 men, wearing my Lanvin black lace. As a woman I took no sort of precedence, being placed several seats away from the governor as befitted my lowly station. Neighbours speculated with some facetiousness what I should do at the end of the meal, and indeed I had wondered myself how I was to get out of the room. Nothing could, in fact, have been easier. As soon as was reasonable after the toast of "The King", Sir Henry left his seat saying: "Mrs Napier, shall we find more comfortable chairs?" and escorted me into the drawing room. It rather pleased me to be told that the nice ladies of Roseau muttered to each other behind jalousies: "I don't know how she *could*."

Committee meetings had their lighter moments, and did not entirely consist of "ponderosities", or even of acrimony and frustration. I remember my neighbour dramatically bringing papers from his pocket to prove a point, and these, having been rescued from an incinerator, disintegrated before our eyes, filling the chamber with a black-grey ash under which we sat silently awed as though a volcano had erupted. On another occasion, the installation of a lavatory for the high court judge having proved unexpectedly costly, it was suggested that the fittings must have been made of gold, and the instrument flushed with champagne. And I remember at a much later debate on the income tax ordinance when a member demanded an increase in the allowance of dependent children on the grounds that he himself had 14, and somebody murmured: "In this house we deal only by the gross."

�**◣**

After the war, when the House of Commons was being restored and all colonies and dominions were contributing gifts, the administrator read aloud to us such a formidable list of proposed donations from other places that he might have been quoting from the Book of Revelations: merchandise of gold and silver and precious stones and all manner of vessels of ivory and of most precious woods, of brass and iron and marble. Everything, in fact, except "slaves and the souls of men". When he had finished, a long and rather embarrassed silence was broken by a senior member of the Legislative Council, a coloured planter. "Considering what we think of the home government," he said, "I would suggest the sending of a silver spittoon." And he stammered slightly as he said it, accentuating the "ssspit".

Eventually it was decided that we should present a silver inkstand, engraved with the arms of Dominica. Whereupon a satirist who then dwelt among us produced (in words) an admirable design, including a "representation of a stack of plans, suitably embellished with red tape and cobwebs, against a background of pigeonholes; the whole to be surmounted by a *crapaud* rampant, bearing aloft a vanilla bean proper, surrounded by praedial larcenists couchant." And concluding with: "In view of the unlikelihood of the inkstand being used as such, the space provided for the inkwell might be occupied by a figure of Columbus, said figure being ingeniously contrived to spring up and exclaim: 'I knew it was all a mistake'."

Administrators, one for each island with a governor for each group, were normally appointed for five years. Sometimes they went on leave or deputised for officials in other places, on which occasions we had an acting incumbent. The word administrator, therefore, must be taken as a generic term, referring to different individuals of varied personalities, beginning with the one Andrew Green described as "born with the instincts of a gentleman but very seldom giving way to them".

We were very much Treasury controlled. The old-fashioned type of administrative officer had been replaced by a puppet pulled by strings from Whitehall. Where, once upon a time a man might act on his own responsibility he now had to cable despatches and consult superiors while his roof was leaking and his foundations carried away. The unravelling of red tape was likely to be a tortuous effort. I remember from my own experience a septic tank leaking at a country hospital. The district medical officer informed the senior medical officer who sent a minute paper to the colonial engineer who passed it to the foreman of works who was sick, and his understudy on leave. Meanwhile the hospital stank and the mosquitoes mustered their battalions.

Again, a bridge on the far forgotten side of the island, and never crossed by a VIP, needed repainting. It would have cost a few pounds. In 1932 the district officer reported this. In 1936, the colonial engineer himself said the matter was urgent. Every year, the magistrate and member of the Legislative Council made duet of complaint. In 1948 the bridge collapsed and, by the mercy of God, with no loss of life. And, for many years thereafter, men, women and little children on their way to school forded the river when the weather was fine. But when the rains came remained on whichever side they might be.

As individuals differed so did the sovereign's representatives. Some would approach the social problem with a touch of hauteur while others sought progress through politics. But all of them seemed to suffer nostalgia for their last post, and were impelled to tell us how this or that was done in Cyprus, in Fiji, in North Borneo.

When we first came to the West Indies, hospitality was dispensed from Government House by garden party. The police band made music under the spreading branches of saman trees. Frilly frocks and morning coats were displayed among gay and gaudy poinsettias on velvet lawns. But soon the ubiquitous cocktail party replaced the more formal gatherings, the last of which took place when a really royal princess and duke fell among us. And then there was so great a scurrying around for gloves and stockings and garters and hats that it was suggested that if everything borrowed were to become suddenly luminous the lawn would resemble a gathering of fireflies or a congregation of glow worms.

It had been recommended in one of those reports actually published and not left choking a pigeonhole that governors should not limit to formal occasions the hospitality which they extended to leading elected members of mixed or coloured descent. This inaugurated an "all boys together" policy, which was not altogether appreciated. During this phase invitations were not, as was customary, sent out for the Government House garden party but a notice was put in the newspaper saying that all were welcome. Staff and housekeeper prepared for ravening hordes, but in point of fact the party was sparsely attended, truck drivers and street cleaners not supposing they were meant to be included; while the middle classes were affronted not to receive a personal card embossed with the royal arms in gold. In these days, when we all tumble over each other to be democratic, it is often forgotten that the common man likes pomp and circumstance, panache and peacocks.

A few days after one garden party I called at Government House on a matter of business and was invited to stay and take pot luck for dinner. The order having been given to the butler to set a place for me he returned wearing an expression of concern. His honour withdrew, and his lady and I made slightly embarrassed conversation till it transpired that the need for another soup plate had revealed the total disappearance of the vice-regal china – white Delft ware, blue rimmed, with GRI, written in gold. Never have I seen cupboards quite so bare, absolutely nothing remaining save the crockery that had been used for luncheon.

The chief of police was summoned; creaking wheels were immediately set in motion, and 36 hours later some 90 pieces, all unbroken, were found buried in the sand of the Geneva river, 10 miles away on the other side of the island. A prison inmate, on the point of release, had been employed – as was the custom – to clean up after the party and, having learned the geography of the pantry, had taken the china and conveyed it by basket and bus over the mountain road, intending to smuggle it to Martinique, from which island, then under Vichy French rule, it would not have been recovered. It was the thief's misfortune that I was asked to dinner before he had procured a boat to take him across the channel, and his folly that he had made a girlfriend jealous who – once the search was afoot – gave him away.

The reasonable employment of prisoners was a recurrent headache. I can remember when they worked in gangs repairing the roads. Then, with the rise of trades unionism, it was argued that a thief should not have a job that might be needed by an honest man. After which you could see a thief languidly sweeping leaves off the lawn at Government House, sometimes passing fruit and vegetables over the wall to a friend in the adjacent cemetery. It was freely supposed that a tunnel led from our overcrowded jail – it was down in the town then – not so much to enable prisoners to escape as to allow them to spend an occasional night at large, returning willingly in the morning to His Majesty's hospitality.

A social welfare adviser once made a report on our prison system after less than two hours on the island while his ship was in transit, and suggested that extra-mural sentences be introduced to relieve congestion. The report came to me for comment when I was recovering from a touch of malaria. "The writer," I said, scribbling in pencil because I was too weak to approach the typewriter, "seems to speak from the stratosphere. His foot never once touches ground." Two years later I was slightly self-conscious, remembering my jibe about the stratosphere written in delirium, when introduced to this same adviser at a cocktail party a thousand miles from Dominica. But he took me completely aback by opening the conversation with: "Your Flying Fish Whispered is the best book ever written about the West Indies." Whereupon I revised considerably my own opinion of his intelligence, realising that here was an individual of perspicacity and discrimination.

That small novel, of which the Manchester Guardian said: "Slight as it is the novel has a unity of form, colour, tone, and texture which makes it a work of art" was published during the Munich crisis and sank like a stone. My first novel, Duet in Discord, appeared on the day of King Edward's abdication. After Munich, my publisher wondered what further disaster I might bring upon the world.

Another social welfare adviser recommended that prisoners be given electric light in their cells at a time when the power house was so overloaded that it was hardly able to function, and a daily meat ration when almost no one in the island ever had meat. Whisper of these recommendations came by the inevitable grapevine telegraph to the ears of the prisoners who promptly went on strike because they were not implemented.

10 | Shortages and smugglers

During Lennox's last summer when he had been feeling the heat at Pointe Baptiste, we bought a small estate on the Imperial Road, five miles from Roseau and over a thousand feet above sea level. Called Antrim, it was an old stone house in the shadow of a saman tree with a purple bougainvillea at the entrance. Actually the property was in the hands of the bank, but nominally it belonged to my son-in-law's cousin who had not lived there for many years. "How about buying my place?" he said to me one day in Roseau. "You'll find it very pleasant of an evening, watching the ships go by." He spoke as though a triangle of sea, two miles away as the crow flies, were Sydney harbour or the Thames estuary. But indeed I did find it pleasant, morning and evening – sunlight on the hillsides and mist in the valley – to watch from the terrace a little sail drifting among cloud shadows, sometimes to be mistaken for a white crane roosting in bamboos.

I put little heart into the buying of Antrim. It was an investment (we had done well from some American shares and with the world in confusion thought it wise to buy land) not a home to be loved. I knew in my heart that Lennox would not live to see another summer. We were told that the house would "do". But when I came to make the house habitable for possible tenants, I found that it would not do at all. Fleas leaped out of the flooring to blacken my ankles. Corners were occupied by chocolate-coloured wood ants' nests. Bats lined the walls, looking like old fur coats that trembled slightly and squeaked. The main part of the house was one large stone room with eight doors, the walls of uneven thickness varying from a foot to 18 inches; and underneath it was a cellar meant to be used as a hurricane shelter. The house may well have been at one time a barrack for slaves, and at the time of emancipation there were 34 slaves at Antrim. Our first tenant claimed to have made friends with the ghost of a one-legged man who went dot-and-go-one in the big room, but I personally never saw or heard him.

Not until the winter of 1940 did I begin to repair and live at Antrim, to explore my property, and grow fond. Suddenly I loved the ragged walls full of maidenhair fern, the royal palms growing straight and tall out of close packed vegetation, the calabash tree with a football-sized fruit squeezed out of shape between two branches. I read in The Golden Bough that some people believe that the soul lives in a calabash, and I thought what a twisted, maladjusted Ariel must be imprisoned in my tree.

Bats hung no longer on the walls but squeaked under the

roof and at dusk flew out from a tiny hole between masonry and rafters. Now and then one or two, lured by the lamp, would circle wildly under the ceiling, sometimes falling exhausted into a corner from whence they might be swept into the kindly dark or, if I could not prevent it, caught horribly by the cat. One I remember, soft-seeming as a mole, crouching beside me on the divan, studying me with an appraising eye. I should have stroked it had I not seen the cruel mouth and known that the bite of a bat can be terrible.

With fuel and tyre restrictions making transport from outlying parts of the islands such as Pointe Baptiste very difficult, it was easier for me to attend to my business in Roseau from Antrim, and more society was available for Pat, who had by then left school. We settled there for a few years and went to Pointe Baptiste only for holidays.

We felled trees, one by one, to reveal others, opened up the sea's v-shaped view, uncovered orange immortelles, the *madre de cacao*, white flowered hogplums and *bois lezard*, with blossoms of a misty blue. There was one unidentified tree, of no especial merit except that it was beloved of bees, which Willy called "Mr-Frampton-he-planted-it-on-purpose." Willy had been the estate's caretaker for 15 years, was growing old, and nothing would dislodge him. I regarded him as gardener and yard man, and he considered himself as manager. "It trouble my health to use a cutlass," he would say. Or: "It is against my nature to burst wood."

On the steep slope towards the stream we planted oranges, whose soft-scented blossoms would catch the first rays of the sun from over the peaks of Trois Pitons; and hemerocallis, the red amaryllis, and a white one from Africa whose name we never discovered, and irises which are not really irises but *marikas*. We added a cassia seedling, which, for three weeks in the year, breaks into the most superb yellow. And as we turned the earth to make this garden, we found it full of broken glass and china, as though the slope had for years been a refuse dump. And one imagined orgies in which bottle after bottle was flung into a heavy darkness under cabbage palms and *chataigners*.

When the house was still unfinished and the garden raw I invited friends for luncheon. Lying on the kitchen table I found a bunch of wild begonias, delicate as Queen Anne's lace. "Oh, Louisa," I exclaimed, "what lovely flowers", coveting them as a table decoration. And Louisa said scornfully: "Madame, that isn't flowers. That is a bush to make a tea for fever."

There were two ruined works at Antrim, one down by the river and the other in front of the house below a great wall held together by ferns. Here there was a relic of a stone chimney, and a rusted iron boiler, which no one would take away. Many such pieces of machinery disintegrated in the forest all over the island: lengths of pipeline from cane-crushing machinery, or cylinders of mills. Once, some of us tried to organise a drive for scrap iron, much against the will of shipping agents and the administration who, I suppose, did not want to be bothered with One More Thing. Inevitably, authority won, seeing to it that no cargo space was available.

So the whole scheme died, Dominica-fashion, and for years little deposits of rusted metal lay on the bay front in Roseau and beside the Indian river in Portsmouth. As the vines closed over the scrap iron, people began to steal away what others had given, playing a game of giant spillikins. The same ingenuity, which could turn a soup tin into a drinking or cooking utensil, could put almost any piece of rubbish to some good purpose. The old signal gun from the bluff near Hampstead, above what was called Bedford bay in the 18th century, was carried to the roadside where it still lies in the grass a reminder of other, older wars.

Massive cannon also lay among the trees on the Cabrits, that peninsular which forms the north shore of Prince Rupert's bay in Portsmouth. (Prince Rupert came to Dominica in 1652, and his brother, Prince Maurice, was drowned in these waters.) Cabrit comes from the Spanish word, *cabra*, meaning goat, and from the sea I have often seen wild kids scrambling over cliffs inaccessible to the rest of us. The twin hills of the promontory were heavily fortified after the Battle of the Saints in 1782, which was fought just round the corner, and there remain beautiful ruins of fort and barracks and governor's residence, where my children and I collected cannonballs for the scrap-iron drive. Those called grapeshot, no larger than marbles, were scattered even in the cemetery where lie the long-ago victims of yellow fever, which was in itself the victor. The fort was abandoned in 1854 and when I first knew it was used as an agricultural station, gnarled lemon trees carrying grotesquely embossed fruit the size and shape of rugby footballs.

When the French invaded Dominica for the last time in 1805 the English governor George Prevost acquired great kudos, a baronetcy and much silver plate – one piece to the value of 300 guineas – for marching his troops out of the burning town of Roseau, across the mountains, and up the Windward coast to Prince Rupert's bay and the Cabrits, from where they held the island for the British. This was a formidable performance, well rewarded. Any modern governor would willingly face invasion, or run away from it, at the same price. There may even have been moments when harassed officials in Whitehall would have gladly paid someone 300 guineas to take Dominica away altogether.

Within a few months of the Pearl Harbour disaster in December 1941, all our pretty Lady boats, the Canadian national steamships, which had served the island for many years, were sunk by enemy action. Thereafter we depended

The Lady boats were passenger steamers that served the Caribbean islands. They were destroyed by enemy action during the second world war.

on sloops and schooners. The Lady Drake and the Lady Hawkins were torpedoed in northern waters but the Lady Nelson met her fate in Castries, the capital of St Lucia. A submarine came into the narrow harbour at night, launched her torpedoes, and retired unchallenged. The look-out man is supposed to have telephoned a warning but was mocked for his pains. "You must be drunk, man. You don't know what a submarine looks like." Tied up alongside the wharf the Nelson sank in shallow water and was resuscitated after the war. But my very favourite piece of encrusted legend is the story of the deaf passenger who did not know until next morning what had happened. Ports were in any case closed and darkened. He had gone to bed early. At dawn he rang repeatedly for his morning tea. At last there appeared a steward saying briskly: "Don't you know we're sunk, Sir?"

Following the loss of the Lady Drake we never in months saw a steamer. Once a tanker on fire dragged herself into Portsmouth harbour with a gaping wound in her side. A Chinese member of the crew was taken into hospital, and someone telephoned to ask me whether I had a Chinese dictionary – a pretty, but vain, tribute to my erudition. When a huge warship zigzagged all morning across the sea in front of my veranda, and then proceeded to make vulgar and alarming noises which were possibly the dropping of depth charges, great confusion was caused among the villagers: those working in their gardens running down to the shore to rescue their women and children; and all those by the sea rushing inland to take refuge from they knew not what.

By now, luxuries had disappeared from our tables; then

followed necessities. The Competent Authority had been conscientious in limiting imports and no reserves had been piled up so there was whining among merchants about their depleted shelves. "War conditions have become well nigh intolerable," proclaimed an elderly gentleman in Portsmouth. Those of us who knew something about the suffering in other countries were ashamed. Watching our children playing in the sea and sunshine, my elder daughter and I felt that we had been chosen of the gods.

After one heated discussion in finance committee about war bonuses for civil servants to meet the rising cost of living, the administrator and I agreed that for the likes of us the cost of living was falling rapidly. We were drinking rum at two-and-something a bottle instead of whisky. It was no longer necessary to entertain with stuffed olives and fancy biscuits nor were we tempted to buy chocolate creams or tinned asparagus. Smokers used a locally made cigarette. But we soon lacked salt and fats and flour, kerosene and matches. Oddly enough matches were more rare than kerosene so that inveterate smokers kept a *veilleuse* permanently burning, the tin lamp which stands in front of a statue of the Virgin, or is used to keep jumbies away from nervous sleepers.

During a shortage of toilet paper, I suggested the framing of a statutory rule and order by which newspapers should be delivered blank to subscribers, for what was printed was indeed not worth the cost of ink. And when I suggested to villagers that having no salt they might well cook their vegetables in sea water they were highly indignant, saying that people in Roseau were ill from so doing. And I believe

Contemporary picture of the newly restored cannons of the lower battery at Fort Shirley, a British military fort overlooking Prince Rupert's Bay and the town of Portsmouth. It was abandoned in 1854. Elma remembered it as a beautiful ruin.

that some had, indeed, taken their cooking water from the effluent of the town drain.

For weeks at a time we had no bread, and never again for many years was flour on sale except to licensed bakers. In vain we argued that a small ration issued to country housekeepers would be an economy for it was possible to make edible scones, as an alternative to bread, out of our experimental banana and cassava flours, but only if one quarter of wheat flour was included. So we devised butterless cakes from grated coconut, and puddings of an incredible stodginess with cocoa and sweet potatoes. Food was fried in coconut oil, which, unless very freshly prepared, was sheer poison to my stomach. What I suffered from "native fry" on my periodical duty visits down the coast was nobody's business. Even fish was no longer plentiful. It was rumoured that U-boats had orders to sink even canoes, so men were reluctant to put to sea saying that fish were now so well fed on corpses that they would no longer swallow ordinary bait. Night after night Freddie Warrington, our gardener, who had replaced both Cozier and King, would come back disconsolate from the bay side. "Nothing like fish," he would say. "Nothing like fish at all."

Eggs were a lively source of friction. The controlled price was five farthings for one, no matter the size. And a village egg was very small slipping down into an eggcup like Goldilocks in Father Bear's chair. "Why they're no bigger than birds' eggs," exclaimed Mrs What-Not with indignation, and we wondered whether she supposed her breakfast to be laid by turtles and lizards. Almost immediately there was a black market egg at tuppence or threepence, which was amusing to remember after the war, when it became possible to pay eight pence. Then there was the absurdity of a regulation by which large eggs had to be sold by the dozen. I can not remember the reason for this but I still have a friend's letter in which he says: "I am hoping that since the best eggs may be sold only by the dozen, milk of good quality may not suddenly become saleable only by the puncheon."

More than the eccentricities of the Competent Authority, we resented the illicit export of our foodstuffs to the French islands. From Pointe Baptiste, very early in the morning, or at dusk, I would see a little boat laden with ground provisions and coconuts and perhaps a small pig, set sail from my own beach at 'Ti Baptiste. This food that we so desperately needed the foolish boatmen would exchange for a cheap and very deadly rum manufactured in Marie Galante. A truck driver once told me, and he was not a man I should have called lily-livered: "If I swallow one mouthful I must vomit." And yet in those times men would spend their days half doped with the foul liquid, leaning vacantly against telephone posts with no strength even to play dominoes. It was not altogether fantastic to suppose that this also, like the crocodile boat on the way to Rio, might be one of Hitler's secret weapons, deployed through his puppet allies to rot guts and brains.

This coincided with the "survivor" period when ship-wrecked mariners occasionally found safety in Dominica. I remember some 20 of them coming to tea at Antrim, men of different nationalities to whom it was hard to make small talk, not so much on account of linguistic difficulties as from awe at their vast experience. And I wondered just how beautiful would be the deep shade of trees, and the cool noise of the river, after days spent in an open boat on a flat ocean oily under the sun, its surface broken only by the drip of oars, by the patterns of flying fish.

When three separate lots of survivors had been cast up on our most hospitable shores, some nice ladies formed themselves into a committee and hired a building, which had formerly been a government office, to make into a clubroom for sailors wherein they proposed to serve snacks, wearing gay aprons embroidered with the letters WW. What those initials really stood for I can not remember, perhaps Warm Welcome, but when somebody's husband pointed out that "white whores" would be exactly what the survivors would want most, the ladies' needles and thread were put to other uses. And it was a piece of "typical Dominica" that, from the time the club was formed, no more sailors found their way to this island. Even so, the rare sight of a fishing sail or even a frigate bird low in the sky might bring a hopeful shout of "survivors, survivors" from excited maidens anxious to be ministering angels.

Later on in the same year, half-eaten bodies were washed up in two or three places on the Windward coast. "Nude corpses, your honour," reported the district officer to the administrator by telephone. And again, 10 minutes later, "More nude corpses." One woman was wearing two medals of the Pope and one of the Virgin Mary, so a Catholic funeral was held of all the remains, but the Methodist minister took care to say a few words over the communal grave just in case some of these pitiful fragments should have belonged to members of his flock. There was never any trace of a boat or lifebelt, although for many weeks crude rubber was found in the sea, and great quantities of white wax. It was not until long after that we heard that a Spanish ship on its way from the Argentine had been sunk in these waters.

News of the fall of Singapore in February 1942 came through in time for Carnival when, for the two days before Lent the people of Dominica run masked in the streets, masked and a little mad, their hands and feet and necks covered so that none can distinguish class or colour, while all dance together singing patois songs to calypso music. The children and I went down to Roseau in a high wind, dust blowing to the sound of drums, waves slapping against the seawall, to find that overnight the people had changed the words of their song "*Hitler, il mauvais*" to "*Japonais, il mauvais*", the phrase echoing over and over with maddening iteration to the shuffle and stamp of feet by people in wire masks – cheeks dabbed pink and eyes blue – through which one might see and not be seen. Some wore old-fashioned corsets or bull horns bound to their foreheads, or robes of shredded rope simulating those of African witch doctors. And the grotesque costumes, combined with the sheer inanity, the utter vacancy of those wire faces seemed fittingly to express the world's cruelty and madness.

One hot Sunday afternoon, I rode five miles on a borrowed mare to explain to the people of Wesley why they should pay their house rate to the village board. Sun blistered my knees, and streaked my steed with dark sweat. The road wound between banks hung with bracken and razor grass from which earth had trickled into drains leaving roots waving in mid air.

My old Morris had recently died pitifully in Roseau. We were no longer carriage folk. I had brought her into town from Antrim for as complete an overhaul as was possible in wartime, and she had been handed back to me guaranteed in working order, needing only a bulb for the rear light which the garage could not supply. A man Michael knew said he could lay hands on one so I told him to fix it, and with crass folly left the key behind. Some hours later he confessed that he had taken the car to test it, to test a rear light bulb on a bright afternoon, and had run it into a bridge "mashing" it up into little pieces. That was one of those days when I did not like Dominica very much.

My afternoon in Wesley was to be another. The village board system of local government had been recently introduced. Members of these boards, nominated by the government, had now been empowered to levy a small rate; and for each pound or penny so collected the government was prepared to give another pound or penny, which sums were to be spent by the people themselves for the improvement of the village. It was thought that this system would serve as an education in self-government. But Dominica could not or would not take it.

Outside the Wesley schoolhouse I found a great crowd assembled but inside there were very few. The arithmetic lesson of the previous day was still chalked on the blackboard. A broken shutter creaked on its hinges. The chairman of the village board was cowering at a desk like a frightened child. An elderly publican said: "I am for you, Madame, but against the board." Another old man told me: "Long ago there was a road tax, and the king was compelled to take it away. Now he would do well to prevent the board from taxing us, for we cannot pay."

The proposed house rate was three pence per room per year. Most houses had two rooms. There was to be no charge on kitchens or outhouses. This was literally a song of sixpence, and no one so poor that he could not sing it. The opposition was a matter of principle. If the village needed improvement it should be done solely at government expense.

The members of the village board (the postmaster, three

shopkeepers, the schoolmaster and I) listened to the increasing clamour of the mob. Doors and windows were closed, but through cracks and knotholes there came enough light for me to see the unhappy faces of my fellows. At last I flung the door open myself and shouted to the louts who, egged on by a few women, were trampling the playground and overflowing on to the road. A nervous policeman gave them here and there a little push with a stick.

"Come inside," I said, "at least listen to what I have to say."

But they replied: "We will not listen. You are our enemy. You have said we must be taxed. You have sold us back into slavery."

"Don't be so silly", I said, stamping my foot. "It will be time enough to talk about slavery when the Germans come."

Then one of the ringleaders cried: "We are not silly, for when the Germans come it is you who will be a slave and not we." This, looking down at the black faces, I thought unlikely. If, on the other hand, the Japanese were to get to us first it might be another matter.

I went back into the school house and, in the half dark, we held our meeting. The schoolmaster read the minutes in a trembling voice. Determinedly I spoke the speech that I had prepared. There was an audience of about 10, including the policeman who had come inside from personal discretion rather than to hear me. My words were barely audible above the rising storm. Some churchgoers from Calibishie were loyally becoming angry on my behalf and spoiling for a fight.

It was obvious that I should leave before worse befell me.

Again I flung open the door, stalked through the crowd, and mounted my horse, almost expecting a stone at my back, which I believe was afterwards thrown at the policeman. I walked the mare away, my head very much in the air, doing an aristocrat-in-the-tumbril act.

Later in the year we tried again. Our own administrator was away in St Lucia, and we thought that perhaps the acting administrator, a man of colour, might be better received in the villages. Certainly he met with no opposition. There was no trouble or ill-feeling. There were, on the other hand, no audiences. All day we toiled and caught nothing. Returning tired and dispirited from our unsuccessful performance of the farce entitled a village board meeting, His Honour came to my house for a drink. There was a letter waiting for me from a friend in another island. "Why don't you consider introducing the village board system in Dominica?" he wrote. "It promises to be very successful here." After reading which we had two drinks.

Next year the secretary of state for the colonies, Colonel Oliver Stanley, informed the governor that he had greatly appreciated the administrator's efforts to stimulate the development and proper activities of village boards in Dominica and added: "It is evident that in this work he has continued to receive great assistance from Mrs Lennox Napier, and I desire to express appreciation of her services also." Which, I suppose, was the equivalent of being mentioned in despatches, and I was duly gratified. But the majority of the people still refused to pay a house rate to the village boards.

The administrator also held preliminary discussion with

the Legislative Council on what was to be another of our failures, the school breakfast sheds. He said: "The governor has been impressed by the efforts made in one of the other colonies to inaugurate a system of providing meals for the poorer children at a minimum cost to the public purse. The school builds a simple little shed, parents and well-wishers give gifts in kind. Cooking is done by the elder girls. A spirit of communal help is built up and a modest beginning in teaching domestic economy is made."

Breakfast sheds were almost as unpopular as village boards. "Cold dasheen was good enough for us," said the fathers, "It is good enough for our children." Mothers told me with anger that they did not send their daughters to school to cook for other people. There was even danger that their contribution, their penny or their potato, might be used to benefit another's child. It seemed that parents resented any domestic or technical education as another relapse into slavery, a forcing of the poor to remain hewers of wood and drawers of water.

One heard, from non-Catholics, that it was the policy of the Church to keep the people ignorant, and from coloured men that Great Britain intended to deny education to her colonial citizens in order that they might be kept in subjection. Both statements were of course palpably untrue, the lack of a hot meal at midday being a far better excuse for illiteracy. Parents seemingly regarded education as a pill to be swallowed and digested without mental effort. If there were no results, then government had administered the wrong pill. Whatever happened, it was guv'ment's fault.

For the breakfast sheds the governor gave me £5 to spend

on cooking utensils in my district. I doubled the gift out of my own pocket, searching Roseau for saucepans and knives and colanders at a time when such imported goods were becoming scarce. (It was a great day when enamel chamber pots were suddenly on sale. Every alternate woman who walked down the street carried one on her head.) I distributed my purchases in the faraway villages of Rosalie, Salybia, San Sauveur, trekking the long road to explain the scheme to schoolmasters. In Marigot, I formally declared open a stone oven and a shelter of sugar trash, where thanks to the headmaster's co-operation, the breakfast shed functioned better there than anywhere else.

What happened to the rest of the pots and pans I can only surmise. Such as were not absorbed into the teachers' own kitchen were doubtless used for the growing of flowers. In village yards you might often see white utensils with rust-rimmed holes, bearing carnations or Michaelmas daisies or plumbago. Only in the convents did the system of school-provided luncheons survive carried on by the devotion and energy of the Belgian-born reverend mothers.

Until 1946, there was no school for Calibishie children nearer than that at Hampstead, a four-mile walk for many of them. One met the little things trailing along the road with their lunch pails of cold roots or plunging into the scrub for a steep and slippery short cut where footsteps notched with a cutlass made, under rain, a series of pools and cascades. Education was nominally compulsory, but already there were not enough places in the schools and so the law was not enforced. (Once upon a time there was a schoolmaster at Hampstead who went to a wedding and next day suffered from a hangover. After opening school he lay down on a bench and told the children he was on no account to be disturbed. And so excellent was discipline that when the district officer chanced to pay an unheralded visit he found the pupils silent and the teacher fast asleep.)

I had long since bought Paul's *moulin* where, in the very beginning we had lodged with Holly. There I established an infant school being fortunate in finding a married ex-teacher with a true vocation who volunteered to instruct the infants if their parents would pay her one penny per week per child. This the people promised to do, and I am afraid seldom did; nor did they pay her in kind, although they frequently paid the doctor so that one saw his car packed with roots and even eggs. I doubt if that good woman ever made more than one-and-three pence a week. Such was her compensation for walking two miles every day to spend five hours, five days a week, hearing little children repeat: "Letter A, letter B, letter C," learn their twice times, and sing songs.

"Does it do them any good?" the development and welfare adviser asked me pessimistically, "to learn the alphabet parrot fashion?"

And I said: "All the good in the world. Fifteen to 20 children are daily washed and tidied, spoken to in English, and submitted to a regular care and discipline while their mothers go to their food gardens." A garden in Dominica might be two hours' walk from the home; or a mother might have to wash clothes in a far river.

A Dominican-born doctor once complained to me that our school curriculum was all wrong. "For instance", he said, "what is the first thing a girl does when she leaves school?"

"Why, have a baby, of course."

His face fell an inch. "*I* was meant to say that," he said. "Your cue was – I don't know, and then I should have told you. Which being agreed, what training do we give her, that she may perform her inevitable function?" And to this I could easily supply the required and expected answer, which was none.

◪

Before the end of 1942 the influx of refugees from the French islands had become almost unmanageable, and a detachment of the south Caribbean forces was sent from Barbados to assist our police. Immediately after the fall of France, there had been a trickle of genuine Frenchmen who had escaped from Guadeloupe and Martinique to join the Free French forces of General de Gaulle. They crossed the channel in rowing boats and we welcomed them as heroes, speeding them on their way. Later the trickle became a flood until it was estimated that at one time 5,000 coloured French citizens were in Roseau, and these not of the best quality. We began to believe that the authorities over there were opening prison doors, saying: "Go to Dominica. You will be fed." It seemed that anyone who was maladjusted, or hungry, might claim to be made part of the Free French forces. I well remember the senior medical officer reconciling it with his conscience to allow a selection of potential warriors to be sent to Puerto Rico for serious training, but after taking one look at it, the American army sent it right back.

Eventually the Free French government in exile recognised that we had a problem on our hands and sent officers of their own to Dominica. The first commander was a Martiniquais of heart-breaking good looks who left behind him a trail of infatuation. I myself was considerably pleased when, after the loss of my own car, he came up to Antrim to fetch me to a Legislative Council meeting, driving me down the hill at Parisian speed in a smart vehicle flying the flag of the Croix de Lorraine. It was said, however, that his ways, which were caressing to the female of the species, savoured too much of the Foreign Legion where his troops were concerned. There was a mutiny, he was assaulted on parade, and had to spend several days in hospital, and was replaced by an elderly French colonel whom we all adored without heartbreak. "*Mes enfants,*" he would say of his rascals, purring like a mother cat, "*mes chers enfants*". One recruit to the French army was found to be 90 years old. "But he can peel potatoes," said the colonel, "he will be very useful."

Our administrator – and it must be remembered that we were feeding these people at some considerable sacrifice to ourselves – drew his attention to "something I never thought to see here, one of our little boys marching beside your troops." "But he *is* of our troops," said the Colonel. "*C'est un brave type.* He will become a cabin boy."

In those days we dreaded riot and epidemic in Roseau. Tenants of small shops and offices had been ejected in order that landlords might line their walls with bunks, one upon another, to the rafters. Behind stone facades there were walled courtyards or a huddle of one-storey tenements now filled with Frenchmen; for anyone who had space to sell for a bed slept himself under somebody else's veranda, or beneath a boat.

Already we were short of food. Now every cow and chicken and cabbage was slaughtered, and the town stank. Twice a day, men in forage caps and a semblance of uniform queued at the communal kitchen, receiving free food and lodging and a dollar a week pocket money.

The Dominica government was refunded by the British treasury which, in turn, was supposed to collect from General de Gaulle. Our man-in-the-street, to whom a dollar a week was big money, found it hard to understand this financial arrangement. The French could buy all the cigarettes, all the girls. Almost. "They fought the dogs and killed the cats, And bit the babies in the cradles, And ate the cheeses out of the vats, And licked the soup from the cooks' own ladles."

There was never serious trouble only because a great many people were making a great deal of money. The French take kindly to a black market. The controlled price of cabbages, for example, was four pence a pound. Someone in the commissariat would sign a voucher for 400lb of cabbages, knowing full well that only 300 had been delivered. In this way control was evaded. Feeding the Frenchmen became a racket.

Not until August 1943 did the Vichy regime in the Antilles collapse, and Admiral Robert was taken into detention in Puerto Rico. Then de Gaulle's army in Dominica was sent home again. The French occupation was over.

One morning I sat in the dentist's chair listening to the sound of men drilling in the street. I could hear: "*Un, de, un, de*", and now and then an unmistakably French bugle call. The dentist said: "The police went on strike this morning. Why? I don't know why. They were out for two hours and then went back."

The dentist was a man with two grievances. A rival from Guadeloupe had been allowed to practise without paying the medical association fees because, it was said, he was treating members of Executive Council free. "Furthermore," and he showed me a paper stamped with the Croix de Lorraine, "today they send me 28 men. How can I treat 28 men in one morning? I am a nervous man. I must work slowly."

A strike among the police was the first of several. The labourers in the public works department came out for higher wages. Nothing of the sort had happened before in Dominica, now coming into line with the rest of the world and trying to organise trades unions. It was reasonable to suppose that if the police struck others would follow. Trades union members had been bribed with the promise of free medical attention, whereupon a stout fellow came to the hospital saying: "What to do for my blood is cold?" meaning that he had become sexually impotent. The doctor told him that it would be possible to give hormone injections but that these would be extremely expensive. "No matter," he said. "Union will pay." And the doctor told me that it did. We could only suppose that this individual was of rare value at stud.

Admittedly there was malnutrition, largely owing to ignorance, to "custom", to knowing best. No labourer need go hungry who had the use of his hands. Everyone, or his sisters or his cousins or his aunts, was farming Crown Land free of rent. But the planter who must pay labour found grievance in the controlled price of ground provisions for it was not possible to grow these at anything but a loss, and so food did not reach the public market. We did eventually raise wages a trifle, and then everyone went on a spree for a fortnight.

Praedial larceny, of which it was said that there would be less if it were called bloody robbery, was the real villain of the piece. A platitude in the West Indies, praedial larceny means the stealing of food from a neighbour: the clearing out of a poor woman's garden, strong youths organised into a band to rob the helpless. Although innocent persons might know who the thieves were, there was no boycott, no punishment by exile from the communal life. The police obtained witnesses with difficulty and if a case were established the magistrates were often known to impose merely nominal fines. Then the word obeah would be in our minds if not on our lips. Nothing so much hampered production as praedial larceny, not so much by the quantity of goods taken as by the discouragement given to cultivation.

Possibly, unethically, I differentiate between stealing from the poor and from the rich. If anyone robs me, which hardly ever happens, I can sympathise with their thinking – she has so much and we so little.

In certain cases there is, or used to be, a code for theft,

indeed recognised rules. The produce of the forest, for example, such as boards and shingles and cordwood, is vulnerable when stored under a house but if stacked on the roadside awaiting transport seemed to be always in sanctuary. When my house at the Chaudiere was broken into and some tins of beef and a bottle of whisky stolen, the villagers were wildly indignant. They might take my mangosteens and breadfruits, cut down my palms to make straw hats and leave the trunks untidily cluttering the river, but to break into Madame's house could only have been done by a foreigner. And indeed the guilty party was known to be an Antiguan, escaped from prison in Dominica and on his way home. He, following his conscience, took nothing but food and drink, leaving behind cutlery and blankets and four shillings in cash.

It was a source of surprise to Holly, who had lived so long in the Pacific, to find no system of chiefs or elders, no headman of the village who could enforce law and order, and punish offences against the community. For these descendants of slaves, the tribal structure had been broken. The Big House, and later guv'ment, took its place. Instead of a chief we had "court". A man dare not denounce a thief for fear of revenge, but there was delight in litigation.

Going to "court" was a substitute for the theatre and dog racing, an alternative to cock fighting, now illegal. To give evidence meant a day's pleasuring at someone else's expense. An unproven will, a squabble about family land, provided endless enjoyable contention. However hard up a man may claim to be, however tight are times, he can always find a penny for the church collection and a guinea for the lawyer.

Shortly after the strike period, Sir Arthur Grimble, the new governor of the four Windward Islands, who had been in office for about a year, came for his swearing-in. This ceremony had been delayed owing to lack of transport. There were no ships, no planes, and an excuse was made that he could not travel by schooner to bring his files, it then being gubernatorial practice to carry the office intact from island to island. And it is faintly funny to remember now that Sir Arthur, who afterwards wrote the book Pattern of Islands and who broadcast so successfully of sea and sail and coral reef, was at that time being accused by West Indian politicians of being afraid to cross the Caribbean Sea.

Eventually His Excellency arrived – upside down – and without his files on the Portsmouth recreation ground. The pilot of his chartered Moth had made two successful trial landings on the only possible piece of flat ground but at the third attempt, with his vice-regal cargo, a puff of wind blew him into a dasheen swamp and the machine capsized. Nobody was hurt. The Portsmouth town board, on parade for the occasion, was able to orate as per schedule.

For reasons known only to themselves, my elected colleagues had decided to boycott the visit of His Excellency. So it fell to me, the junior member, to make the speech of welcome in the Court House. Lights had been improvised, but the rows of faces at right angles to me were almost indistinguishable. His Excellency was very late. I became more and more nervous. "Himself has been nearly dead," the administrator suddenly whispered from behind me, giving me a five-word briefing on the Portsmouth landing. When the oath had been taken I stood up in the dark. I had intended to indicate that Sir Arthur was several months overdue by saying, "We are glad to welcome you here at last," but on hearing of the crash I graciously changed the last two words to "this evening".

When I had finished, my neighbour whispered, "You did that beautifully," while the governor made a stiff little bow and said, "Thank you." So began a friendship, which I am still proud to remember.

11 | Deck Class to Barbados

People were beginning to go mad. A black doctor, mistrusted and unjustly suspected by his clinic patients, literally cried on my shoulder, weeping real tears, because someone had called him a chocolate pudding. A magistrate with wife trouble opened his veins but was prevented from dying and sent down to Barbados under medical escort. A young mother of four, dreading an increase of family, suffered frustration to the point of horror. This was a state of affairs not altogether new in Dominica. It had already been said that instead of building a lunatic asylum we should make a small enclosure for the sane. Before my time there had been the misogynist major who had shot intruders on sight; the distinguished botanist who died while digging a hole through to Australia. Now we began to look sideways at each other, wondering: "Will you be the next? Or I?" There was a woman who was in love with somebody else's husband, and she knitted him a white woollen sweater to be worn after tennis. At the club he proudly put it or for the first time; and had proudly worn it for no more than a minute when someone said: "Moths get into it, what?" And when he looked down at himself he found that the wool had been deliberately and ingeniously cut in a thousand places. This, I think, was as sad and sorry an exhibition of wifely jealousy that I ever heard of, lacking the dignity of murder or even of scratching out the eyes.

In the summer of 1943 I had not been out of Dominica for two years, and had been facing, as who in those desperate years had not, personal troubles. In the previous autumn my elder son had been killed in the air during the German raid on Canterbury. In the year before that Michael had been mysteriously ill, but had recently returned to Barbados to continue his education. Pat, who had left school on taking her School Certificate just before the loss of shipping made education a parent's nightmare, was unreasonably, alarmingly, frail. It was time to get up and go.

In those days one travelled by schooner, or one stayed at home. On the fourth of June, Pat and I took passage for Barbados on the Gloria Henrietta, a little vessel thought too insignificant to be attacked by submarine or machine gun. We had, as fellow passengers, those courageous and constantly seasick women called hucksters, or more curiously, "speculators", who carried our fruit to sell in other islands, making the voyage over and over. When we came on board we found their cargo littering the deck, and our own luggage did nothing to lessen the confusion. The mate, in thin torn sweater and felt hat said, "Everything stays here until security has seen it. Then we'll stow your things in the hold." Security officers were a feature of the times, men apparently selected for their knowledge of oriental languages, or for their ability to strike oil in Peru, who were sent to the West Indies on mysterious avocations and, finding little else to do, quickly developed an infinite capacity for propping up bars. The ship's captain was still on shore. Someone said: "It isn't navigating that makes a sailor nowadays. It's getting your papers fixed."

We sat on our boxes for a full hour. It was so still an evening that smoke rose straight into the sky to make a thin mist over the river. Flags hung heavily at the fort and from Government House garden there was an occasional cackle of hens making ready to roost in mango trees. "Security" made us open every item. "Democracy, democracy," he muttered through his pipe. "I must examine your luggage as thoroughly as theirs." When the inspection was over sails were hoisted and the dinghy hauled on board.

The sun had set in a red haze. An American corvette which for some reason unknown had come into the roadstead that morning started with a flourish of her screw that would have been insulting had not her wash pushed us a few yards further from the shore. The hucksters supped noisily. There was exchange of badinage with the crew, sometimes a snatch of song. Schooners carried no form of sanitation. When it was fully dark a communal pot was handed round but not offered to us. Democracy did not extend that far. Pat and I had brought calabashes. We spread our mattress aft and lay upon it thankfully, maintaining our position for four nights and three days. Men stepped on us occasionally, when doing whatever it is that men do to boats, but never painfully. Upon our first midnight I was awoken by the noise of creaking spars, which is comparable to that of a sawmill but lacking rhythm, for they grate and squeal irregularly, the wind keeping time no better than a slate pencil in the hand of a moron child.

We had drifted with the current to Scott's Head, that tiny peninsular also called Cachacrou, on the south-west corner of Dominica, which is attached to the mainland by a strip of sand and manchineel trees. Now for the first time we were meeting the breeze of the Atlantic. The boat rolled to a slight swell. By the light of stars, mountains were blackly outlined. On such a night, three half centuries ago, ill-disposed French inhabitants of Dominica had entered the fort on Cachacrou to make the soldiers there intoxicated with liquor, and afterwards to fill up the touch holes of the cannon with sand. When the enemy from Martinique stormed the fort next morning it was easily taken, and for four years Dominica suffered under French rule.

By nine o'clock we were generously to windward of Martinique. Already the heat was almost overpowering. The volcano was hidden in cloud but sunlight illumined pale cane fields and the rim of surf under the cliffs. Whenever we sat up to see the scenery immense green rollers, passing so surprisingly under and not over the little boat, were sufficiently disturbing to our stomachs to suggest that we lie down again and let the scenery be. Every two hours came an order to pump ship, and then men manipulated a creaking handle.

That night the sun set behind St Lucia. I made friends again with the Southern Cross, but to find the Great Bear I must sit up and crane my neck. By morning there was no sign of land and the sea much rougher. Twice, waves broke over us, making the hucksters laugh from the elevated position on the hatch, where there was a risk of death from a swinging boom if they should raise a head at the wrong moment. For a little while after our soaking we experienced a most excellent coolness, but soon our clothes were dried again to the consistency of salted board. At noon a plane passed, a silver speck almost imperceptible; this we knew to be the St Lucia to Barbados mail and greatly envied, for to be cool and swift was all our desire.

Few things in human experience are more boring than schooner travel, with the sun blistering or the rain pouring, and the motion precluding reading or conversation or even coherent thought, and the sea being empty of shark or whale or porpoise or submarine. When an ex-governor of Barbados referred in a broadcast to "picturesque schooner travel in the Caribbean", I wondered how much more he had seen of it than the tangle of spars and rigging in the careenage. Now and then we sipped water or Brand's Essence, our chicken falling eventually to the ship's pig. Schooners always carry a pig for the accepted reason that if a crew loses its bearings, and the porker be thrown overboard, it will instinctively swim in the direction of land.

Late in the Sunday afternoon men began climbing masts to look for Barbados, a small flat island easily mislaid. Recently a sloop had sailed backwards and forwards over the place where the captain thought it should be and, having found nothing, reported it sunk. I visualised missing it altogether, sailing on and on until we came to Africa.

Again I woke at midnight, to so great a silence that I supposed we were totally becalmed. My mind being still on Africa I asked the captain sarcastically as he tripped over the mattress: "Have we come to Dakar yet?" And he said: "Yes, we reach." Turning, I saw Bridgetown behind us, and found that we were not becalmed but anchored outside the net or boom, that antisubmarine device of wires and steel buoys which would not be opened for us until dawn.

The Gloria Henrietta was anchored indeed but not very securely. And it is amusing to recall that, having had so much trouble in locating Barbados we should in the end hit it, drifting on to the reef with a horrible grinding noise, and taking on a considerable list. Making one sweep with his great paw the captain gathered us up, baskets, water bottles and all, and ladled us into a doghouse, one of those kennels with curved roofs that housed him and his mate, and kept us cooped there until daylight while he manipulated sails and oars and eventually extricated his vessel from her lopsided and most uncomfortable position.

Trollope described Barbados as "a most respectable little island". The shopping centre is called Broad Street because it is so narrow, and the road leading to the most chic suburbs had no sidewalk but only a deep drain. Old barracks converted into flats and stained red; emerald lawns between the yacht club and the sea; bougainvillea in half a dozen shades together with scarlet flamboyants and blue plumbago bring pleasure for eyes wearied by the glare of limestone. Beyond the town, cane fields reminded me of young wheat, and, for a moment ignoring the avenues of palm trees leading to estate houses, I could fancy myself back in north-east Scotland. There was even a lighthouse well placed to suggest the one near Lossiemouth on the Moray Firth, and I remembered with unusual nostalgia those wild rides on the sand with my dead brothers.

Barbados, as did everywhere else, suffered during the war from restricted transport. In order to go shopping after breakfast you leaned against a telephone post, at the foot of which the house next door had dumped its garbage, waiting for a bus and hoping for a pick-up which one in three times happened. Few things seem so cruel as a half empty car passing with supercilious bonnet when you are hot and in a hurry and hating your feet. In the bus you wedge fit yourself, six to a seat, among fat black women with baskets, or coloured soldiers, or other islanders on their way to beaches. Everyone was friendly, cheerful, with a ubiquitous: "Yes, please."

We had come for a six weeks' visit to Barbados, which represents, to the small islands, Harrods and Harley Street, Eton and Roedean. (A Barbadian woman told us: "You in the other islands are so lucky," meaning exactly the opposite, "We never need to travel.") But, in the event, we were stuck there for five months, and it was nine before I was able to return to Dominica.

Pat was accused of having a shadow on her lung, and although no one was ever quite sure how seriously ill she was – and by great good fortune we were able to have first-class advice – with her father's history we could not afford to run risks. Europe and the United States were closed to us; but there was a government sanatorium in Jamaica. For admission there we had to apply to the Executive Council of that island, where on top of everything else my letter was mislaid so that we waited and waited in desperation, and for the first time I experienced insular claustrophobia. I knew the rat-in-a trap feeling although I was suffering this benevolent imprisonment among kindly old and new friends.

On the last day of October we set out for Jamaica by air, stopping off for a few days in Trinidad to make the connection. Trinidad was an anything but respectable little island. Those were the days of "zoot suits" and "robust boys", of food queues in the slummy streets where Chinese, East Indians, negroes, whites, were all trying to beat the black market. The popular calypso of the moment began: "Small island boy, go back where you came from" directed at those who, from Grenada and elsewhere, had sought work in Port of Spain.

Water buffaloes wallowed in rice fields no bigger than billiard tables, and of the same colour. Pomeracks showered the roads with purple blossoms. And on the golden-flowered immortelles, I saw the immense nests, shaped like the wind indicators at airports, of the birds called yellow-tails. Looking to the northern ranges I remembered a Trinidadian high court judge who had once taken tea with me at Antrim and who, finding it cold at 1,200 feet, had kept putting on and taking off his little coat. "But surely you can go up to 3,000 feet in Trinidad," I said, irritated by his fidgeting. Whereupon he replied repressively: "We can, but we don't."

For the first time in years I travelled by train in Trinidad, and in the night heard the whistle of locomotives and the clanking of braked cars. The governor had removed the chairs from the vice-regal compartment and was sitting in them in Government House because, he said, nobody used the railway any more. Nobody – except, at dawn and dusk, hordes of black and brown and yellow clerks and typists, shop assistants and labourers, and, at midday, enormous red-faced men in khaki and slightly paler ones in white ducks. In the Queen's Park hotel, American soldiers and sailors waited, open-mouthed, for the golden gates of the bar to be opened, while some slept hideously on the leather couches, recovering from the last hangover, anticipating the next.

The windows of commercial aircraft leaving Trinidad were blacked out in case spies should count the shipping in the Gulf of Paria. When the Pan American steward put an end to this blind man's buff, we were flying over the delta of the Orinoco, as dreary a waste land as I ever saw, a network of stagnant water and grey palms wherein Sir Walter Raleigh had once sought Eldorado and found only, "White cranes and red herons and crocodiles, and Indians who dwelt in trees, and drank bones powdered in wine." There were five airports in northern Venezuela and we came down in all of them; and the further west we travelled, drawing out time to catch the sun, the more red and arid became the landscape until the plane fled from it over the sea, leaving behind a rampart of mountains under cloud. That night, at the hotel in Barranquilla – from where we proceeded to Jamaica by seaplane – boiled potatoes were served with every course on the elaborate table d'hôte menu, and we sampled every course for the sake of the potatoes.

I loved Jamaica on sight, almost as long ago I had loved

Dominica. From my hotel I looked to the high mountains, clear and cool and sharp against the horizon. Every afternoon on my way to visit Pat in the sanatorium, I walked through paddocks where cattle grazed among flowering trees and crossed a dry ravine with steep sides wherein I once disturbed – not very seriously, for they hopped and flopped and stood to watch me – a dozen of those huge black bare-necked birds called Johnny crow, and in Trinidad corbeau, which are not crows but unashamedly vultures. In Port of Spain I had seen them rising hideously from the abattoirs to line fences and telephone wires as might swallows in a kinder, softer country.

Transport was an even greater problem in Jamaica than in Barbados. To wangle a car ride was an adventure. Some people had even exhumed horse buggies and fitted them with rubber tyres. I was incredibly lucky to be given, through a development and welfare introduction, a four-day trip into the western parishes by a member of the agricultural department who was investigating farmers' unions. For this I had to pay, very inadequately, by making speeches on small-town platforms, talking of Dominica in places where the eastern islands were hardly known, even by name. There were no tourists in those days. I saw the North Shore beaches empty, had Montego Bay to myself.

Just before Christmas, there was a headline in the Jamaica Gleaner: "Crisis in Dominica Legislative Council". Elected members, opposed by the nominated element, were pressing for a general election. The representative of the Northern District had walked out of a council meeting and resigned his seat. The Gleaner's correspondent said: "With the previous resignation of the member for Roseau on grounds of disagreement with the policy of the Administration, and indefinite absence from the island of Mrs Napier, elective representation in the Dominica Legislature is now reduced to one."

Pat had settled down and was a little stronger. She could safely be left in kindly hands. In any case I could not have afforded to stay longer. I secured a Pan American passage for early January. Two days before I was due to leave, my flight was cancelled on account of someone else's priority. In those days any GI on a spree might throw a civilian off a commercial plane no matter how urgent her business. I cabled my plight to the governor of the Windward Islands who arranged a priority for me with the government of Jamaica. I have seldom been as proud of anything as of that (fourth class) priority.

Noel Coward, who had been recovering from flu in Jamaica and was now en route to sing to soldiers in Africa, was the only other through passenger to Trinidad. He wore a doughboy's uniform, and the pretty Pan American hostess at Barranquilla airport could not make out who or what he was. Bewildered by the presence of the British consul, the expensive luggage, the camelhair coat, she said: "You must be Somebody. Why don't you wear badges, ribbons?" Mr Coward answered, "Because the colonel wouldn't like it", and I murmured the song of another war, "Would you rather have an eagle on your shoulder or a chicken on your knee?" Looking back after boarding the aircraft, we could see the girl still watching us, open-mouthed.

Barranquilla from the air gave that tiny but erroneous

impression of being a toy village. Patches of cassava and okra, sunken hovels, stucco cathedral, even vultures, all blended into one picturesque whole. The Magdalena river had brought forth silt to make new lands on which mangroves sprouted like stubble on an unshaven face. Far out at sea there was a line, clear-cut and definite, where the yellow power of the river ended and beyond which the Spanish Main was indigo. Soon we flew among mountains, almost brushing the plane's wing with snow that was pink in the sunrise. From a great height I am often reassured that the world is not so overcrowded as statistics make out.

From Trinidad I was again given air priority, returning to Barbados via Grenada. Michael came down from school to spend the weekend with me in Bridgetown and developed measles. For three days he was seriously ill and we were quarantined together for three weeks. I came back to Dominica by schooner again, at the beginning of March, only just in time to fight the general election that only about three people wanted.

N

At home I found censorship established at a time when, with the departure of the Free French, all real need for it was over. Hitherto, the postmaster had opened such letters as he thought looked interesting, each week holding back, to read at his leisure, a different subscriber's copy of Time magazine. Soon after my elder daughter's appointment as chief censor, the head of the group organisation requested her to have her staff photographed for the benefit of headquarters in London, and suggested that while she was about it she might send along a picture of a West Indian schooner. "Good idea to let those chaps at home know how we have to travel."

A few days later, our local photographer, who normally dealt in wedding groups and passports, was brought to the censorship office, under arrest, by two policemen. "Mrs Agar," they said to my daughter, "can it really be true that you ordered this man to photograph the harbour?" (An empty sea stretching to the horizon, terns and boobies perching on the bamboo anchors of fishpots, tiny waves slapping the sand under the seawall.)

Censorship might be a bitter thing in small islands where the secrets of our hearts, of our bodies, of our finances, were at the mercy of people we met at cocktail parties. The appointment of personnel from overseas made little difference. Within a few weeks they were absorbed into the community, were au fait with local interests and gossip. On leaving certain islands, all books, business documents and magazines for the journey had to be taken to the office for censorship, although you might wrap your boots in any newspaper you chose. And I remember seeing at Trinidad's Piarco airport a pitiful shrunken old man open a shabby trunk full of nothing but newspaper cuttings and old letters, one would suppose the accumulation of a lifetime; and there were tears on his cheeks because they must all be checked and approved and there was no time, no time.

Only once to my knowledge was a letter of mine mutilated. Michael wrote me from school, "What on earth have you been telling me about Alice-pig which has so annoyed the censors?" I wondered whether complaints about our food situation had brought comfort to the enemy, and remembered saying that we loved Alice so much that no matter if we were starving we would never eat her. Not until a year later when he showed me the tattered fragments of my letter, did I recollect that we had watched a blimp from the Pointe Baptiste veranda. "Everybody ran to see it," I had written, "even Alice-pig."

In one of the larger islands, censorship sought to control not only military and naval information but also the general tone of correspondence. When a girl we knew was "in trouble", someone wrote: "Poor Gladys. I suppose it was an American at the base?" And the word American was cut, presumably because such a suggestion could not be made about a noble ally. Praise of a Brahms symphony on a postcard was returned to sender with the comment that it was inadvisable in these times to express pleasure in German music. A lady who had attended a girl-guide rally at Government House wrote to her sister: "The mean things only offered us lemonade." Which criticism of His Majesty's representative was not allowed to leave the island. It would have been difficult, in the circumstances, to make a complaint to the governor.

12 | Manners, migration and bananas

We were at Antrim when the news came through that the war in Europe was over. Pat and our servant went down to Roseau to join in the celebrations but I stayed alone, wandering rather aimlessly in the garden, picking and arranging flowers, and feeling strangely tearful on account of overweening memories. The day happened to be Lennox's birthday. Far away on the hillside a goat was crying. From the saman tree there came a great clamour of birds. Clouds resting on Morne Trois Pitons were puffed off by the wind as might a man blow froth from his beer; as might peace blow trouble from the world.

The coarse scent of marigolds was on my fingers when suddenly, from behind a bank of lilies, appeared my henchman Willy with a strange female dressed all in black. "She seek a remedy," he explained, picking a brown thistly weed to add to a bunch already collected. And he told me, "I hear that my daughter make a man-child." I duly congratulated him, but for whom or for what was the remedy I did not know.

That night there was an impromptu dance at the club. The girls wished to invite some of the English Royal Engineer sergeants who had, for several months, been making, or trying to make, a map of the island. But the club secretary would not permit this because the men were only non-commissioned officers. A curious overture, one would have thought, to our World-Made-Safe-For-Democracy.

In 1946, I set foot in 19 different countries or islands, and spent much time in the air venturing to Europe, with Pat, for the first time in seven years. In Cambridge, we visited Michael, who, although coming often to Dominica was never to live here again. Pat, too, stayed in England but only for four years, eventually working for the British Council. She came back to me in 1950 and was married in the following year. Both of them gave me grandchildren to be my delight and pleasure.

When I flew back alone from London to the West Indies at the end of 1946, it was via Amsterdam, the Azores, New York and Curaçao – a 52-hour journey, to Barbados. From there, it was another 52 hours to sail home.

As we drew slowly alongside Dominica in the Endeavour, crew and hucksters sang very delightfully in the twilight. There were calypsos and Christmas carols, and "brown skinned gal, go home and mind baby". Then the cook tuned up from the stern with:

Leave her, boys, leave her

Leave the old Endeavour.
The rice boil away and the saltfish gone,
Leave her, boys, leave her.
One by one the crew took it up.
Leave her, boys, leave her
The galley overboard and the mainpeak down

And each one improvised some new calamity. And not so long afterwards the old Endeavour did sink, and I doubt if anyone regretted her.

So I came back to the peace and the quiet and the loneliness of my own veranda. Mountains stood darkly against the sunset. I heard again the mournful cry of doves. Robert the donkey pulled on his chain because he knew I would come down to give him a banana, to kiss his velvet nose. The dog called Jack, last of the Calibishie crabhounds, barked at his heels from sheer jealousy. Freddie brought his bucket to the tap below the terrace and Alexa joined him to watch the little fishing boats making for the passage in the reef.

I knew beyond doubt that it was here I wanted to live, and to make ready to lay my bones in that quiet place under trees.

◥

After 12 years in my service Louisa made a good marriage in the village and retired. Cozier died just after the war when he had already been for a long while on pension, towards the end suffering from dropsy and outgrowing all his raiment. At that time there was no "pyjama cloth" in the island, and we could only procure a very gay and girlish cotton with which to make an elephantine nightgown. I found there was something appropriate to his personality that he should have gone to his death and almost certainly to his grave, in this unusual not to say garish pattern.

A few years later Clifford quarrelled with me seriously over the Calibishie village board. When the police, after a year's patience, came to distrain on his fishing boat because he still refused to pay his house rate, having been ordered so to do in the magistrate's court, he came screaming into my garden waving a cutlass in my astonished face.

"They may put me in prison for seven years," he said "They may cut off my head. But I will not pay village board."

I remembered his passionate outcry during our house building. "The people of this parish," he had said, "are the wickedest in the world." Now it was the government who was wicked, or I. Not so long afterwards he went to sea in his boat and was caught in a storm and drowned. Then I thought of the little song he had made long ago when planting my garden: "This will surely live. This one cannot die." And I was very sad.

For a little while after Louisa there was Jane, a flamboyant character who one morning woke me at dawn with the most piercing scream I ever hope to hear, running into my room to take refuge from an ex-lover who pursued her with Guadeloupe scissors, which for some reason are larger than ordinary ones. It seems that he had lain all night under the servants' house in order to obtain first-hand evidence that she loved another. In the morning, prepared to kill her, he politely refrained from so doing in my presence, and meanwhile her paramour slipped away through the bay trees. I, who had thought my house isolated, was amazed to find how many neighbours gathered in answer to that scream, running out from the little wooden shacks on the road to Paul's *moulin*.

Murders are no more frequent in Dominica than anywhere else, but there is often a twist of originality to the tale, something of what Alec Waugh called "Typical Dominica". During the war, an old eccentric took a gun into the hills above Antrim and sheltered in a cave, from whence he shot an intruder whom he accused of spying. (Doubtless there was the usual notice written with a charred stick: "Trespassers will be persecuted.") In those days it was customary for the jury in a murder trial – segregated from friends and family until the verdict was given – to be taken for an evening drive at government expense. With serious tyre and petrol shortage it was decided on this occasion to practise an economy and omit the drive, and the jury were so angry that they deliberately brought in a verdict of not guilty to spite the administration.

More recently another murderer escaped into the forest with his gun. Then for many weeks the neighbourhood went in fear. The man, who went crazy whenever he had taken a drink, had not killed the person at whom he had aimed, but an innocent bystander whose father appealed to me – in vain – for government compensation on the grounds that the guilty party had already served a sentence for manslaughter and should never have been let out of prison. Fruitlessly and at great expense the police scoured hills and valleys. And at last a skeleton was discovered, conveniently near to the hospital, lying beside the hunted man's gun and shirt. Two bones, the jaw and a broken clavicle, by which the doctor might have identified the murderer, were missing; but the island felt that honour was satisfied and called it a day. Suicide in the circumstances would not have been unreasonable. But few people in the north were ever convinced that the wretched boy had not escaped to Puerto Rico or Guadeloupe, deliberately leaving his shirt and his gun beside unknown bones. For a long time it was supposed that he came home at Christmas to visit his mother.

In every society angry passions rise, and the ubiquitous cutlass is a handy weapon. But I have found the people among whom I live – a blend of French and Carib, of English and negro – to be a kindly, friendly people (except perhaps in the heat of an election). And a polite people, for alone I have walked on the country tracks, bathed in sea and river, ridden the windward coast to sleep in derelict estate houses or in primitive police stations, and always met with civility. Night or day it is possible for a woman car driver to pick up a passenger without greater risk of meeting trouble than that of showing him how to open the door. Should an old man make the sign of the cross on entering that is an instinctive gesture, and not intended to show distrust of her skill at the wheel. For years I have lived alone at Pointe Baptiste and never closed door or window, except against the weather. (Long light nights under the moon, with the sea roaring. Swirl of rain on the roof, and water running in the gutters. Sometimes a ship passing. Sometimes a man fishing by *flambeau* from the rocks and the flame reflected on the walls of my room.)

Dominicans are a generous people. The descendants of slaves like to give presents to white people, be it only a sweet potato or roses. Looby said: "When I have a fish I will give it to you." And as I protested, knowing his poverty: "Well, Madame, when I catch two fish I will give you one." In our village, breadfruit and the common mango were never for sale. "Oh, no, Madame, that is not to buy, that is for you." Or, "Madame, you have only to ask."

When we came to the island we found that customs and manners varied from one village to another. The people of Calibishie, for instance, would never milk goats, although one was tied to every tree, and the kids pranced in the high road. "Use goat's milk, Madame?" someone would say in a shocked voice. "Oh no, Madame. In Vieille Case they milk goats but not" – said with civic pride – "in Calibishie." During, the war, together with a coloured doctor and the district officer, I tried to encourage the consumption of goats' milk to the extent of persuading the government to purchase an Alpine buck that was circulated for service in the villages. But no one was very interested, perhaps not even the animal, and the process became inevitably known as "passing the buck".

In the beginning, every day held some new adventure, some phenomenon of weather or cloud formation, some new beast of the sea or flowering tree, some funny letter or an amusing turn of speech. "My man is dead," said Mrs Blackman, "please to give me a little cash." Robert wrote: "As I have not heard from you, so I thought it best to remind you as I know that such small trifles may have slipped your memory. Things are very brown with me at present." Inevitably I now take much of this for granted, and such interruptions to work or social intercourse have become matter of routine.

Often I have been exasperated by the absurd superstitions, the political arrogance and ignorance, the insistence that "guv'ment" do everything, give all. I remember a moment long ago when, on my way home from a rather thankless expedition down the coast, I sat to rest myself on the veranda of a friendly tailor who was treadling his machine. Someone produced a penny bread and I ate it with my last piece of cheese, watching a small lizard puff out its yellow throat. Under a broken step there was a crab's claw, smothered in ants, and a small snake hiding behind a corn cob. And I thought – why must these people grumble so much when there is not a poisonous reptile in the island, nor any wild beast to snatch their children, where the sun shines and the rain falls and there is no great heat nor great cold? But I understood well enough in my heart that to be truly happy one must have known worse things.

Four years after the war prosperity discovered Dominica. In 1949 an Irish company, Antilles Products, set up a new business in bananas; and although everything did not go smoothly in the beginning, and the promised fortnightly shipments were often delayed, so that when my sewing woman asked me: "When is next fortnight?" I had to give her the equally crazy-sounding answer of, "Not for six weeks again," money trickled through to the peasants and then at last began to pour. Within a few years the little

The dining room at Pointe Baptiste, with a screen painted by the chef Marcel Boulestin.

village stores, smelling strongly of salt fish, where dabs of orange butter (from coconuts rather than cows) were gouged on to a tin and wrapped in old newspaper, had olives and cream crackers on their shelves, gin from England and whisky from Scotland. One could buy, without going to Roseau, American cigarettes, and tinned milk, and scented soaps. The baker, using the same little stone oven, could change a five-dollar bill twice in the week. Soon there were several bakers, and far too many rum shops. In the village at night one heard the bawling of a radio and the thrumming of engine-charging batteries. Progress was the order of the day.

Bananas are not such an ornamental crop as cocoa, whose golden and green and crimson pods hang like jewels in a dark shade; nor even as coconuts, sprawling over the sand or standing straight and tall in the fertile valleys. Often banana leaves are torn to shreds by the wind, and sometimes they turn yellow from diseases called Panama and leaf spot. But when they shine like silver plates in the moonlight or when raindrops roll off them like balls of mercury, then they have a beauty that is all their own. The plants are not reproduced from seed but by suckers, which sprout round about the old stem. The cycle of growth takes about nine months. From above those rather vulgar flowers – gross purple petals with a satin texture and a red lining – there develop bunches with an average weight from 20 to 60lb. These are cut when green, whether they are destined for export or to hang in the kitchen to ripen.

Neither peasant nor planter was immediately aware that bananas for the overseas market must be handled like rare wine and not tossed light heartedly into lorries from off a man's head. To begin with, a trash carpet was laid in the trucks. Later, plastic bags for wrapping were distributed. But these made the packing and storing of our personal effects altogether too easy, so the management perforated the bags with holes the size of halfpennies. At the ports one saw women carrying bunches swathed in rolls of plastic, as long ago other women carried coal into the bellies of ships in Port Said or Kobe or Castries. For 150 years things had gone surprisingly wrong in Dominica. Could it be true that something would now go right?

Food became very expensive. Our cost of living was higher than in other islands. The ships which brought us our imported goods could not come alongside the jetty and so cargo had to be landed by rapacious boatmen and porters,

Bananas became a commercial crop in 1949 and fortnightly shipments to the UK brought some prosperity to the island.

whom one could hardly blame for demanding high pay when the ships came so rarely, but the costs fell squarely where costs always do fall, on the consumer.

"What to do?" cried the storekeepers, "What to do?" And there was nothing to do. Stephen Haweis, the artist, said of the shops in Roseau: "They find out what you like so that they may never order it again." And there was the tale in circulation of the two old ladies who sometimes stocked unusual things, including on one occasion packaged rice which people appreciated. But a customer asking for more was told: "Oh, we're not ordering that again. It moved off the shelves too quickly."

Money poured into the laps of the peasants yet there was malnutrition as never before. Such was the enthusiasm for this "green gold" that the small planter with enough cash in hand for his own needs would hardly trouble to grow his own food, let alone carry to market surplus provisions to sell. Were his wife lazy, or weak, unable to work her own garden, children went hungry. No one was the healthier for consuming gin and white bread instead of dasheen and mountain dew. One could no longer hire a man to mend one's house or repair one's shoes. Carpenters, masons, schoolteachers, domestic servants, all were "behind their little bananas".

But the green gold had a noticeable streak of brass in it. I have always deplored what I understand by "the American way of life", the compelling of a man to work by titillating his women by shiny advertisements. But I have seen the antithesis create its own problems. No one was instigated to extra labour by desire for a streamlined kitchen; for exotic deodorants or a new line in brassieres. If the sale of a few bunches per fortnight would supply a man with tinned beef, why should he keep a cow? Why not sit in the sun and catch crayfish? Or just sit in the sun? The rushing past of overloaded lorries, the disputes around the weighing machines, all made for sufficient entertainment. The dirty note or the solid silver kept the planter as happy as the shelves crowded with canned goods kept the shopkeeper. But to export all our food in order to import all we ate seemed a curious policy. Those of us who were supposed to exercise some sort of control, to consider economics, found the situation bewildering.

Of course it was not everyone who sat in the sun, and almost nobody caught crayfish. Bananas became very much big business, and money was made on the sidelines, much of which went into housing and even more into motorcars. One noticed the change in small ways. Calibishie people had hitherto walked five miles to church on Sundays bearing grips and shoes on their heads, and waiting after mass for Vespers, so that they might come home in the cool of the evening. Now two trucks were not enough to accommodate those who could pay for a seat.

When a rather shabby man on a clattering cycle asked to see me privately and my mind reacted in the old way with: "How much is he going to beg from me?" I was amused to find that on the contrary he was wanting to buy my car. Of an evening, men played bridge in the rum shops – I had, by request, sent down a volume of Culbertson, the contract bridge expert – or listened to the news. My dresses were not begged from off my back any more. I could wear them to a ravelling myself. No longer was there a complicated list of IOUs in my cash box.

Instead, there was endless matter for happy contention over the amount of tax to be paid to the Banana Association; about where and how and if fertilizer should be made available; about spraying against diseases; about the monstrous sums of public money mysteriously lost by those handling the buying and selling. It was safer not to understand too well the web of intrigue woven by banana politics.

The flight to England in the 1950s was not, as in larger islands caused by economic necessity due to overcrowding

GRIMALDI LINE

T. V. ASCANIA

CALLING AT DOMINICA

ON 27th AUGUST

for

SOUTHAMPTON DIRECT

Third Class Passage – $312.00

Inclusive of Taxes

Messrs H. H V. Whitchurch
Agents

)180 –3 AUG.—8

*Advertisement from the Dominica Chronicle, 1957. The
era of migration to the UK began in the mid-1950s.*

and unemployment. We were seriously short of labour. From
Dominica it was not so much the down-and-outs who
emigrated but much needed craftsmen and government
employees. Teachers and policemen – trained at the state's
expense – fled to dig ditches, or to close doors on the
London Underground. The thing was as crazy as the rushing
of Gadarene swine. The head teacher in our village begged
me, "Speak to the people, Madame. Advise them not to go."
But I said: "Who am I to speak? I left the country of my
birth to live in yours." For I recognised the sense of
adventure, the desire for change; even though it meant
change from beauty and a soft climate to the slums of great
cities. Travelling from Kensington to Hampstead I have seen
from the top of a bus, late on a Sunday morning, men in

their dressy clothes pouring out of those peeling, half-stuccoed houses near Paddington, and been amazed. It was as though some invisible Pied Piper had whistled them on to the great ships.

Sometimes they asked for money to help them go. There was the pitiful policeman, who told me that he had collected the cash and then lost his wallet, offering me as security half a house in Portsmouth in which his sister worked as a seamstress. He pretended not to understand that I could never want half a house 13 miles away, nor turn the woman out to sell it. And the carpenter working at Hampstead who claimed that his father had voted for me: I had walked down from the Chaudiere in teeming rain hurrying against a rising river. Water streamed from my hair, and I could hardly lift my feet for the mud on them; and then found that my car, parked under a windbreak, would not start. At this singularly ill-chosen moment, the man pattered after me down the road, pleading for his passage money. And all the comfort I gave him was to ask him to push the car, which he obediently and successfully did.

I was exasperated by the light-hearted ignorance with which they set out. There was that other carpenter, planning to leave at the New Year. I begged him, "Wait at least until the spring." But he told me: "No Madame. It is not cold in England in January. Only in December." Pat's husband Ted gave an old windbreaker he had used in Canada to a boy who wrote: "Sir, only when I come to Plymouth did I understand what it was for." Sleet and smuts and stuffiness were taken in exchange for sea spray and the scent of orange blossom. But many of our people seem to have found Eldorado. A great deal of money has been sent home, as formerly from Cayenne and Curaçao. In one day the postmaster had to send three times to the bank for more money to cash postal orders, and the queue stretched all round the building.

A few years ago I bought new china at Harrods. Weeks later when I unpacked it I found curled up in an eggcup a little note: "Mrs Napier, just to tell you this was packed by a Barbadian boy."

13 | Battle of the Transinsular Road

In 1947, almost all of my former constituents signed a petition asking me to come back to them, to represent them again on the Legislative Council. This I agreed to do. A gentleman in Calibishie congratulated me on my faith and gravity, and the West Indian Times referred to the good works and human exhibits displayed by Mrs Napier and her late husband. Hitherto, as a member of the Legislative Council, I had not been paid, but now I found myself in receipt of £100 a year, which my colleagues had voted themselves in my absence. Two years later there was another increase. "I must pay a man to carry my basket," piped my neighbour. "I must give a friend a little cigarette."

Again in 1951 there were elections, for the first time under adult suffrage, but I had already told my people that, on the brink of 60, I could no longer face those long journeys on foot or by horse to the windward coast. Then the government once more offered me a nominated seat and

Elma Napier on the Legislative Council, 1951, following the first election under adult suffrage.

this time I accepted. So from 1951, for yet another three years, I sat at the blue baize table, marvelling that nominated members should be paid the same salary as those with a constituency to look after. It was all so easy, with the stream of visitors stayed, the voluminous correspondence abated. No longer did I have to pay a man to carry a basket, nor reward a friend with a little cigarette.

Yet we worked much harder on my later tours of service. "Finance committee every fortnight?" jeered a newcomer from one of the African colonies. "You must deal in chicken feed." Very likely we did, but chicken feed is important to the fowl. Every fortnight from Pointe Baptiste, because

Antrim was let for a long period, I drove for three quarters of an hour to Portsmouth and then spent from three to four hours in the public launch, always fearful lest there be a puncture and we arrive late. (In Dominica any breakdown of machinery is a puncture, not only the disinflation of a tyre.)

Often I would leave in the early morning, at moonset or sunrise. Sometimes rain would beat down the valleys and the rivers run yellow, carrying refuse of trees caught up in a grey froth; and sometimes the ocean would be so flat and oily that flying fish dripped v-shaped patterns as they skimmed the surface. Then the water would be bottle green under cliffs, and you might see sunken rocks smeared with ochre, and coral mushrooms, and white clouds reflected on the ocean like columns of snow. And once, for some reason now forgotten, there was a night journey when flying fish were coated with phosphorus, and it was as though luminous butterflies idled before the bow wave of the boat.

It was while I was a nominated member that we fought the battle of the Transinsular Road. I suppose that from the day the first car was imported, there had been talk of making a highway through the mountains. In 1700 Père Labat had written: "We walked right across the island to the windward coast seeing nothing more interesting than trees." (And I was wondering what could be more interesting?) But Dominica was still two islands and not one. From time immemorial the Caribs had used a trail crossing the watershed between the Pagua and Layou valleys. The French wound their *pavé* around it, making the grade easier. At a lower level there was an English trace. Lennox and I had

Elma supported the building of the Transinsular Road in the 1950s. Here, the demanding work progresses in the interior.

walked the Carib trail when it was still blocked by huge trees, victims of the 1930 hurricane, when Père Labat's trees had been flung about like match sticks. We found that in order to surmount the vast trunks, travellers had cutlassed footholds in the fallen timbers to make ladders.

In 1941 the administrator and I accompanied the first comptroller of development and welfare to the northern terminus of the road. For lack of a bridge, the "pitch" ceased abruptly at a place called Deux Branches. Labourers' barracks were crumbling to pieces. Barrels of surplus cement had been rendered solid and useless by the damp. "All we have to do now," said the administrator, "is to find a way over that mountain." It would have been tactless to point out that he was indicating an altogether wrong mountain.

In 1944 our development and welfare department, in

answer to our importunities, authorised the completion of the road from the southern end. Once I went up into the far interior with the junior engineer – the same one who, when invited to renew his contract, refused saying: "No social amenities in Dominica, and those there are I don't like." Where a grass track had been there was now a wide cutting metalled with jagged stones, raw and newly broken, waiting for a roller to crush and colas to cover them. The truck wheezed and lumbered painfully, protesting, that such anguish should never be asked of tyres and engine. Where a few years ago we had walked in the twilight of trees there was now a bare hillside strewn with axed stumps, half hidden already by razor grass and wild eggplant. Here and there an immense root, extracted by giant forceps, lay indecently exposed by the road's edge. Where we had once forded the river, thigh deep, keeping our feet with difficulty, there was a new concrete bridge, defying storm and flood and swirling logs.

The main camp, christened Norway by men who found it so cold working there, was half a mile further on. The engineer had a two-roomed house with a chair, a desk, a bed and a wireless set. On one shelf stood ink and iodine and a bottle of whisky; and on the other a basin and the glass for measuring rain. (The average of inches per year was working out at 270.) There were half a dozen one-roomed shacks and a barracks called by the labourers a "long house", a very hideous erection of untrimmed saplings with a galvanized roof. Between all these lay the road, a ribbon of squishy yellow clay printed with the marks of bare feet, in the deeper of which water lay.

Sometimes a board, or a series of boards, served as a pathway through the muddiest sections. As I rather specially made use of these, the engineer mocked: "If you like, I'll tell off a man to lay boards in front of you all the way." It was Sir Walter Raleigh stuff, with a board for a cloak.

Fifty feet below us the Layou river made a series of alternating pools and rapids. A hundred feet above, immense trees were bound together by vines and lianas. Here the road was a shelf sliced from a precipice; and here, when the great rains came, the trees fell and taking with them soil and rock and fern swept the road into the river so that there remained only a grey and yellow scar of supreme ugliness.

From all over the island men had gathered to work on the road. Some had walked 16 miles from Roseau; and some had begged lifts from lorries, swinging the zigzag track which ends in the hardpan country, the *terre faim*, where nothing good can grow, but only fantastic trees so burdened with parasites that it is hard to know where branches begin and epiphytes end. On this section of the road, early in the 20th century, several English families had settled. Now one may search in vain for the foundations of their houses. Here and there a red hibiscus has survived, or a vivid cassia.

Men crowded into the camp asking for a job, carrying sacks or baskets containing a week's food. One said to me: "Look how a lorry mash up my tin," showing me a piece of crushed metal that had once contained four gallons of kerosene. "Now I have nothing left in which to cook my little provision." The overseer asked him: "You want a job? You have tools?" There were not enough tools on the island for so many. No bulldozers. No shovels. A road that elsewhere, or in other times, would have been driven through by adepts with engines was given to inexperienced persons armed with toothpicks. Men excavated stumps and boulders by pickaxe; women headed away earth on wooden trays, bare-footed, carrying soil from one hole to put into another.

A few months afterwards it was announced that there was no more money. The whole £50,000 grant had drained away. Some said the labourers had killed their own golden goose by working too slowly; but there was also woeful talk of feathered nests and of wilful (profitable-to-someone) waste. The next engineer said: "We can't let this stand as a monument to British inefficiency."

Patiently, for eight years, the administrator and governor worked to persuade higher authorities to make another grant. I myself went to the Colonial Office in 1949 and again in 1952 to put in my humble request. And at last the money was given. Development and Welfare scheme DI776 became an accomplished fact. At the end of their terms of office, the administrator and the governor left to take up other posts, confident that Dominica would soon be one island instead of two.

And then, in the course of nature, there came to us a new governor and a new comptroller of development and welfare. The new administration had been with us for less than a year. They did not know the background, and had not shared the long years of failure and hope. Without precedent, finance committee was summoned to meet on a Sunday morning. Country members had been told that it was not necessary to attend, but I happened to be in Roseau anyway.

At this meeting a member whose interests were confined to another part of the island informed the governor that in Dominica it was no longer considered desirable to build the Transinsular Road and that the money would be better spent otherwise, or other where, thus launching a thunderbolt that was not only totally unexpected but as regards half the population completely untrue. Without pause for thought or comment the governor, metaphorically waving a blue pencil, said in his breezy way, "Well, if you are all agreed?"

I took a deep breath and said, "No Sir, we are not agreed." A few days later the administrator announced in a press release that "he took full responsibility for the sudden decision to postpone the completion of the Transinsular Road and that he proposed shortly to ask the legislature to agree that allocated funds be diverted to the construction of a road joining Roseau with the eastern coast."

In finance committee I had been alone but I was not alone for long. The north was unanimous in its indignation. At village meetings people said, "Madame, heaven will bless you." A monster petition was prepared for presentation to the governor. Every evening a table was set out in each village, and the people came at dusk to put their names to the paper (or their marks), women in their working clothes, men from fishing or from "behind their bananas". A 223-word personal cable was despatched to the secretary of state for the colonies, and a question was asked in the House of Commons (I had it on good authority that the Colonial Office was scared stiff of questions).

Elma Napier commemorated on a Dominican stamp. She was the first woman to sit in any West Indian parliament.

Then a mass meeting was organised in Marigot, on a day when all shops were closed for the occasion, and no work was done on the estates, where some 3,000 people assembled of whom perhaps 500 were able to come within sight and sound of the speakers. And so a few months later another official notice was unostentatiously published saying: "It is now proposed to proceed with the construction of the Transinsular Road." But the why and wherefore of this obstructionist policy, which held up not only the road but the making of the airfield for nearly two years, was never made clear to me. Graft in high places? Administrative fear of disaster? The Curse of the Caribs? It happens in Dominica.

I was not actually in the island when the road was opened to traffic. I understand it was not so much opened as rushed. For weeks anyone who could find jeep or truck forced their way across in one direction or another. I myself happened to be in Ankara, where the snow lay heavily on the mountains, and the frosty air was so keen that I could hardly breathe it. In Turkey, American aid was paying for wide smooth highways where American cars rolled at an easy 70 miles an hour over the bare Anatolian plateau. There could be no greater contrast than between these and our twisted ribbon of a road, threaded among the dripping sinister trees of the virgin forest. When I came home in January 1957, and was driven for the first time where I had so often walked, finding the land still raw from its cutting; streams imprisoned in culverts; banks of red earth pockmarked by rain and already eroded into small pinnacles of mud, then I was overwhelmed by an awesome sense of responsibility. But when, a year or two later, I was no longer on the council and not thinking anyone remembered I ever had been, our chief minister said to me casually at a cocktail party: "After all Mrs Napier, it is your road." Then I was childishly proud.

14 | The sea for company

The fabric of memory is woven of scraps and patches. It has not been given to everyone to hear a coffin made over the telephone; nor to make a bonfire of bamboo and hear the hollow trunks explode like gunfire; nor to be caught by a tangle of thorny creepers called *arrete neg'*. For the matter of fact, it is unusual to see a kingfisher born. Michael and I were in the kitchen at the Chaudiere when a man brought in two eggs for my son-in-law. We put them on a saucer and thought no more about them. An hour later we heard in that place, where no cat could be, a kitten's cry. Treating this as a delusion we nevertheless heard again the strange mewing and, turning at last to the shelf, saw a scrawny shape struggling to divest itself of a cloak of soggy eggshell. And it haunts me to remember that we could not reach the nest to put back the nauseous thing, but had to leave it at the foot of the river bank, praying that the parent birds might rescue it somehow before a rat came, or a snake, or the yellow land

Elma on the red rocks near Pointe Baptiste, 1949.

crab called *cyrique*. And we never knew the answer. In the morning, there was nothing there.

I was alone at the Chaudiere, superintending the re-shingling of the roof, when I heard that George VI was dead. Before noon the news had travelled up the swollen river by grapevine telegraph; and the head carpenter, the man who eight years before had stood beside me in Vieille Case when the people had shouted me down, climbed off his ladder and stood before me saying: "Madame, this is a sad day for us, for it seems that our king is dead." Then a little group of negro peasants gathered in my kitchen to talk with tears in their eyes of a man whose pain was over, and of a young girl flying from Africa to become Queen.

A year later I went up to Roseau to receive with a dozen or so others the Coronation medal. At six-thirty of a fair morning my Prefect died under me on Blenheim Hill. There was a rending noise from the clutch and she would not move again. That is that, I said. No car, no medal, no Government House party. Suddenly from the opposite direction a forest ranger arrived on his motorcycle. I turned him round, climbed up behind him, and so rode pillion into Portsmouth, arriving just as the launch had cast off, and doing a frantic dance on the jetty until it came back to me.

"Did you leave late, Madame?" said George the porter. I could have wrung his neck. As though I ever left late. This was the first time I had ridden pillion, and I thought that Her Majesty, had she seen me, clinging bare-headed and bare-legged to that portly frame in the saddle, might well, unlike her great-great-grandmother, have been amused.

◪

Of all the powers and pleasure old age has taken from me, I most regret my strength to penetrate the forest, to revisit loved places. I shall not see again those canary-yellow rocks, grotesquely smeared with sulphur, in the upper pools of the Picard river nor climb that staircase in stone which leads precipitously from the Jaquot flats into the gorges of the Layou river ("Slave labour?" pooh-poohed an elderly inhabitant. "Mr Campbell built it 50 years ago.") Nor shall I ever dare the 'Ti Trou in the Roseau river where the cliffs so nearly meet overhead that one struggled in the swift-flowing water under no more than a sliver of daylight, with the howling of frightened dogs echoing and re-echoing like the cries of the damned. There was a great *chataigner* tree under Morne Diablotin, its trunk buttressed by a dozen flanges taller than a man. I do not know whether it is still standing. Nor what happened to the fig (my henchman called it a "milk tree" for the texture of its sap) in the heights above Antrim, whose python-like roots undulated on the surface for many chains, holding *balisier* and razor grass in fearful embrace. Then there is a place called Battissements, in the very centre of the island, where runaway slaves, allying themselves with Caribs, had made habitations and food gardens. There we found lianas thick as a man's thigh carrying stored rain water, which the peasants knew as *corde gleau*.

I still crawl to the Chaudiere where once I pranced, passing through a green twilight of bananas newly planted under the coconuts. The grass with the speedwell-blue flowers, which we call French weed and in patois *zeb gwa*, rakes luxuriant knee-high growth in the dark shade of green acquired from the artificial fertiliser now in general use. "Walk well, Madame," the people say with a smile, men and women carrying coconuts, or a boy changing his cow. And again, anxiously: "Madame, the river hold you back." It is not the river to blame for slow progress but the advancing years.

The peasant has no respect for non-commercial plants, and I seldom have strength to "make a round" of my property, or else let fatigue be excuse not to discover things of which I do not approve and cannot prevent. Now I prefer to do needlework among the red amaryllis, watching a heron on the rocks beside the Centre pool, listening to the four musical notes of the *gros-beak*, or to the warning of rain from the *coucou manioc*. Sometimes the smell of the river seems to carry with it the breath of the forest's decay, and sometimes a rock is rolled by flood into a new place, and then my ears can detect a new sound in the water, and the shape of a fall is altered. And always I am aware how fortunate I am to be able, on the brink of 70, to go to the Chaudiere at all.

Many people, often strangers making it the object of a drive, have been in and out of this house, propping themselves against the veranda rail to breathe their ahs and ohs, asking: "How did you find it?" or "Do you really live here alone?" Patrick Leigh Fermor gave me that lovely write-up in his book about the Caribbean, The Traveller's Tree. ("Dug-out canoes?" Paddy cried rapturously as we chugged up the leeward coast in the public launch, "how madly Robinson Crusoe.") Alec Waugh, who many years ago described Dominica as the most beautiful island in the world but the most unlucky, has been a more frequent visitor – and has even returned to find the bad luck broken. Peter Fleming, commissioned to do a West Indian article for Holiday, breakfasted here en route to the Carib Reserve but said no more of this island than: "Dominica is the place to go to if you are an ornithologist, or if you like eating toads, or if you are a connoisseur of rainbows, here sometimes visible by moonlight, or if you want to visit Caribs..." Charles Morgan, the English playwright and novelist, with the shadow of death on him, stayed for a fortnight with his wife, the Welsh poet Hilda Vaughan. But he was too tired and she too absorbed by the shade and colour of mountains to write anything.

Then there was Ann Davison, the first woman to sail the Atlantic alone in a sailboat, sick and exhausted from her journey, she arrived barefooted and serge-trousered in the streets of Portsmouth having made her landfall in that once-upon-a-time whaling station. And Adlai Stevenson, also barefooted but from bathing, making me promise never to sell the blowhole rocks without first offering them to him. And Noel Coward, after "an enchanting day" wrote of "this curious magic island".

Once upon a time Princess Alice of Athlone peered through lorgnettes at my Gauguin reproductions and inquired whether they were the occupation of my lonely days. And a few years later, while I myself was abroad, another more highly publicised princess spent a day of her honeymoon here, arriving so smothered in flowers,

Princess Margaret drives through Marigot on way to Pointe Baptiste.

presented by enthusiastic villagers, that she and "Tony" could, only with difficulty, get out of the car.

Persons from other islands, making fun of our frogs and of our excessive rainfall (my own record has been 12 inches in one day, in which six fell between breakfast and lunch) are faintly jealous of that certain something which lures unusual people to our shores. Long ago, painters and bird lovers and misogynists came here to live quiet and inexpensive lives, but since the last war, with the cost of living so high, that does not happen any more. Yet it was in the late 1940s that an elderly gentleman from Yorkshire tried to make his home in Calibishie and died of starvation, not owing to lack of cash, for I found 300 dollars lying in his trunk, but because he was a confirmed vegetarian. Our villagers seldom grew "English" vegetables, and spinach and grapefruit are like patriotism, not enough. A few months later a woman from California drifted to the village and found lodging, refusing to meet me because I had servants and she had none. "Come to see my white lady visitor," her hostess begged me. But the Californian ran away among the trees, and soon afterwards died also.

In the summer of 1948, the Rank Organisation, filming the first landing of Christopher Columbus in the New World, treated us on Woodford Hill beach to the most monstrous picnic of all. Then 200 people of a dozen nationalities and almost as many avocations – wardrobe keepers, hairdressers, property men, continuity girls – swarmed over a beach where normally there were only crabs and sandpipers. For a fortnight sun blazed on sweating, bearded sailors dressed in serge tunics. For a fortnight longboats swayed and tossed to the sea's movement. At a given signal, furious activity of oars would bear them forward with a sweep of waves into which Columbus would leap to make a landing. Sometimes the ocean would miss cue and the boats would come broadside on, wallowing in confusion. Sometimes the stand-in actor would lurch or stumble, sinking too deep in sand or sea. And on some days the surf was less heavy than on others. The continuity girl, slumped in a deck chair behind a jug of lime juice and two pineapples, could not control the beat of the waves or the cloud formation in the sky.

Meanwhile Caribs, brought daily from the Reserve, climbed with bows and arrows among the seagrape trees, which the camera man insisted on calling dingleberries. "Taffy," he would yell to a man with a saw, "rid me of these dingleberries." Or sometimes: "Bring me dingleberries", to be a frame, to create a shadow. And Taffy, thankful to break his idleness, would obsequiously hurry forward with a branch of round glossy leaves and pinhead-sized fruit, which I never see without remembering the giant camera under its green umbrella, the reflectors swathed in mosquito netting; the waves of shimmering sand-heat dowsed by buckets of seawater. We had never supposed that our Catholic Caribs would so readily undress, and had visualised reverend fathers rushing into the picture waving mother hubbards. But they moved about the beach, brown, naked bodies chequered by sunlight and leaf shadows, in specially dyed loin cloths as unselfconsciously as a Folies Bèrgere chorus. Few of them had ever been to a cinema. Nobody knew what the sequences meant, what it was all about. But they knew what five dollars a day meant in terms of rum and cloth.

Columbus never really set foot in Dominica. He never discovered it until his second voyage, making his original landing in the flat and scrubby Bahamas. But the director said, "We'll take poet's licence on a mountain. After all, scenic effects are expected of the West Indies." He would not, on the other hand, let the Caribs be painted with the crimson *roucou*, as was their ancient practice, because the public would suppose this to have been invented for Technicolor. No poet's licence might be taken on grapefruit or banana skins, on bathing suits or sand shoes. Columbus' sailors drank coconut water no more than Coca-Cola. Before every "take", actors, doubles, extras, must rid themselves of cigarettes and dark glasses and, for that matter, of negroes.

On the road, beside the river, our villagers sold hardboiled eggs and pineapples, even crayfish or a fowl and much money percolated, like rain after drought, into hidden corners and valleys. Then we learned an altogether new language. Danger money, drawn by those going to sea in heavy armour; lunch money, which meant five shillings a day for union members whose contract provided for a knife and fork meal at midday. In the old "works", where limes used to be crushed or sugar, sandwiches and Cokes were served. Three hundred bottles of Coca-Cola per day, and no one ever seemed to have an opener, so that bottles were jerked against trees and rocks and reflectors, even on the very legs of the sacred camera. And I remember thinking that bottle cans would lie forever and forever in the sand until the day when the New World was rediscovered by

*Elma with her grandson,
Lennox Honychurch,
1952.*

some new Christopher Columbus, perhaps from another planet, after the next Dark Ages.

Within 18 months it came to be believed that Columbus really had landed at Woodford Hill. The movies had made it so. The estate changed hands, and the ruined works were restored in the name of big business and the banana. Warehouses were replaced by garages, copra dryers and cattle sheds. But the sea seemed to take exception, for it battered the land and tore away trees as though in angry lust to reach the concrete walls. Soon there was no place for

Columbus to have made a landing, only have a beach on which to set foot.

Once, when I gave a talk on BBC radio's Woman's Hour, I described incidents in my life as a member of the Legislative Council, piling on the discomforts, the oddities: remembering sleeping in police stations where the rats took my food, describing how the governor on his way from the Carib Reserve was unable to cross a flooded river so that my dinner of frogs and flying fish was wasted. A few weeks after I met a man who was starting up a new business in Dominica. "I've got a bone to pick with you," he said, "on account of your broadcast one of our wives won't come." She did come eventually, of course. What is more she stayed.

To live in Dominica it is not necessary to ford flooded rivers. There are more things to eat than frog and flying fish, although nothing so delicious. It was Henry Nelson Coleridge, nephew of the poet, who took such startling objection to the crapaud when he visited Dominica in 1825. "It is the most unbearable beast I ever saw. I can hardly think of it now without being qualmish. I can eat monkey, snake, or lizard; there is not much in that; but verily to munch, or crunch and squeeze...gah! It is downright cannibalism and popery." (The last two are surely a curious combination of epithets even for an ardent Protestant.) Mr Coleridge objected to crapauds for esculent reasons, but had he known what I only learned recently, that these toads practise birth control by eating as many of their own young as they can catch, he might well have protested on moral grounds. Not even I advocate such means as these for the reduction of population.

I have never eaten, nor been offered monkey snake or lizard, but I have tasted agouti, which I did not like, and shark, which I did. Salt fish, basic luxury of the West Indian since the days of slavery, I cannot abide; but it was across a luncheon table in Nairobi, of all contrasting places, that I once met a parliamentary representative of New Brunswick, whence salt fish is exported, and we shed tears together over the recent withdrawal of the Canadian national steamships, the consequent falling of this trade important to both of us, his constituents being on the producing end of the trade and mine on the consuming.

I went to Africa in 1954, to a conference, in Nairobi, of the Commonwealth Parliamentary Association. It was Dominica's turn to send a delegate to represent the Windward Islands. Nobody else wanted to go. When I piped up that I should love to, my offer was accepted, even with the suggestion that the island would be grateful. The Mau Mau campaign, then at its height, had put Kenya on everybody's map. "Give my regards to General China," puffed one member from behind his cigar. "Mrs Napier, I should never dare," said the government clerk who arranged my passage. Just before I flew away, I gave a lift to some linesmen employed to clear branches off the telephone wires. One said: "Madame, it seems that you have to go to Africa. We shall indeed pray God until you return."

Although the conference itself was held in Nairobi, where

Family and friends, 1952. Back row: Percy Agar (son-in-law) with Elma. Front row (left to right): Penny Narodny, Elizabeth Agar and Antony Agar (grandchildren), Ted Honychurch (son-in-law) and Patricia Honychurch (daughter), Daphne Agar (daughter), Mary Narodny.

I spoke about the marketing of West Indian citrus, in that curiously cold but austerely beautiful chamber in the parliament buildings, we were invited to make additional tours through Uganda, Tanganyika, and the Rhodesias, being treated with rare munificence. The occasional terrors are long since forgotten, terrors not of wild beasts or wild men but of speaking in public, of being conspicuous, of being late. The kindness and good fellowship are unforgettable, not only of Africans but of professional politicians gathered from every corner of the globe. Friendly intercourse between the peoples of the Commonwealth – breakfast with New Zealand, lunch with Ceylon, dinner with Pakistan, and a car ride with Sierra Leone made perhaps the most valuable part of those exercises.

The year 1954 seemed to be an important moment in African history, with the Kabaka of Buganda in exile and his people at odds with the British governor; the Central African Federation embarking on perilous seas, the world full of fear that the Mau Mau movement might spread. But it is all rather small beer nowadays, when everything is more bitter and more confused. It was difficult to make anyone, black or white or copper-coloured, understand how differently situated are the races in the West Indies. Kikuyu, Kipsighi, Baganda, even Maasai, crowded eagerly to ask: "What are the Windward Islands? And why? What do you grow? What do you do? How many people are there? Are they educated?" To the average East African child, the average Dominican one would seem to be very well educated. A woman in Uganda told me parents feared that if a girl had education she would not find a husband; men saying: "She will want to eat eggs", which was apparently the equivalent of our grandmothers' demands for a latchkey and the right to vote.

Newspaper reading, here and now, is more comprehensible to me for having seen the copper belt. I can now distinguish between Baganda and Buganda. I know what the Lukiko is, remembering that rather church-like building with a thatched roof and white-washed walls, surrounded by an intricate and beautiful wattle fence, which is the parliament house of the Kabaka.

Elma Napier on the veranda at Pointe Baptiste in 1960.

Our final banquet was held beside the Victoria Falls. I found mail waiting for me at the hotel, including the results of the latest elections in Dominica, and the not unexpected information that I was not asked to sit again as a nominated member. (I had made quite a nuisance of myself over that road.) I was too tired to care very much. Dominica was a long way from the Zambesi. The island seemed very small and unimportant. The roar of many waters, the twittering of strange birds in the tree outside my window, dulled any sore feeling there might have been. I knew that I had done a good job in Africa. It was better to go out with a bang than a whimper.

I had been chosen to make the last speech, to strike the final note by thanking the peoples and parliaments of Africa for their wondrous hospitality. The Dominions each had their own speaker; but the colonies, the pinpoint islands and the scattered territories, were to be represented by a woman from the least important of them all, selected, doubtless, because she was not likely to arouse jealousy. (Surprisingly enough the statesmen were jealous, often very much on their dignity about their personal and territorial rights. They positively squabbled to make speeches and shouldered their way into photographs.) When, after a long dinner and many words spoken, I rose to say goodbye and thank you, knowing that I should never again take any part in public life, I made reference to the good times we had had in Africa by saying how strange it would be to go back to an everyday existence: to pay for one's own taxis, to take one's own tickets, to go to perhaps one party a month instead of three every day. I hoped that nobody would come to earth with too big a bump...

They were all very kind to me that night. Jim Griffiths, secretary of state for the colonies, told me: "Damn good speech, little girl." A coal miner from New South Wales said: "You must have been a lovely lady when you were young," and a senator from South Africa countered with, "She's a lovely lady now." But when I came back to Dominica nobody cared who had spoken for the colonies. The roar of the falls could not be heard in Roseau. The smoky mist rising from the gorges of the Zambesi did not stretch across the Atlantic. Only the women of Calibishie village, bringing me presents of yams and eggs and roses, said: "We are glad to see you, Madame. We thought you would be eaten in Africa."

Nowadays I live alone in the house and like it. At first this was not easy, but I have learned to appreciate solitude as one of God's gifts to humanity. Unless I have guests, I dine as it grows dark. Then the servants go about their own business and the house is mine. Often I fall asleep early, and wake at midnight to prowl the veranda, or watch the moon rise out of the eastern sea. The bright lights of Marie Galante may still be shining and occasionally I see headlights on the other side of Blenheim bay where the new road is advancing towards Vieille Case. Lennox never knew these evidences of "other people". Progress marches on both sides of the channel.

Should I be hungry and visit the pantry with torch wedged into my armpit to leave both hands free, the cats leap upon me from no matter where, crying for their tidbit, and I realise that although I may think the house is mine, so do they. When I sit down to my meals with book or paper propped before me there will be a sudden thud of falling feet on the table and a greedy paw will come round the corner to steal from my plate. The younger has a habit of walking in front of me rubbing its head on my ankle. I prophesy, here and now, that I shall die of tripping over the stupid creature. There is no dog any more. When Jack died, who was born of an unknown father in a copper *taish* in a neighbour's yard, I knew that I would never again expose myself to such unnecessary sorrow.

Day and night I have the sea for company. As Kipling wrote, "The heave and the halt and the hurl and the crash of the comber wind-hounded.... His sea in no showing the same..." Sometimes pale blue and glassy, streaked by currents; or indigo, flecked with white horses. Sometimes – a trick of the sun – bottle green with purple stains where reefs are, or, in bad weather, filthy with mud when rain makes gutters of the seams in the orange cliffs and the rivers spew forth their quota of eroded soil. After a night of exceptional storm I have see my whole world blood red, as though the sun were rising through crimson gauze. Sometimes, every valley and mountain top will be close and clear as though I could touch them, and within the hour they are grey-shrouded, with the sun throwing broad rays from behind cloud, as though the Holy Ghost were descending from heaven.

Inevitably, there have been changes, but perhaps fewer in this mysterious, sensational, sometimes sinister island than anywhere else in the world. The cost of living has soared out of sight; political conditions are different; communications are more convenient. But my view – that great stretch of sea with a background of faraway mountains – has not changed although to keep it I must constantly wage war on encroaching vegetation and sometimes lose my battle. Trees rooted on the cliff face have defiantly thrown up branches, which are beyond man's reach to cut. I have had to remove shrubs Lennox planted because they grew too high. But the infinite variety of light and shade on Morne aux Diables is still there for my pleasure.

There is the same intimacy with sea and surf. Foam

smothers the grey islet a hundred feet below the terrace. Spray from the blowhole drifts westward like a puff of smoke. Every morning, as in the beginning, a kingfisher rattles his way towards the reef on White Beach. Towards evening, as in the beginning, a fish hawk swoops over the red rocks casting a purple shadow, and, in the dry season, the air is filled with the sound of doves.

Index

Lightning Source UK Ltd.
Milton Keynes UK
UKHW04f1508200918
329231UK00001B/21/P